Leadership in Christian Higher Education

Leadership in Christian Higher Education

Edited by

Michael Wright and James Arthur

imprint-academic.com

Published in the UK by Imprint Academic
PO Box 200, Exeter EX5 5YX, UK

Published in the USA by Imprint Academic
Philosophy Documentation Center
PO Box 7147, Charlottesville, VA 22906-7147, USA

ISBN 9 781845 401894

A CIP catalogue record for this book is available from the
British Library and US Library of Congress

Contributors

Professor James Arthur

James Arthur is Professor of Education and Civic Engagement at the University of Birmingham and was formerly Professor and Director of the National Institute of Christian Education Research at Canterbury Christ Church University. He has written widely on Christian education and his recent books in this area include: *Faith and Secularisation in Religious Colleges and Universities* (published by Routledge in 2006) and *John Henry Newman* in the Contiuum Library of Educational Thought (published 2007). He was awarded a CBE in December 2009.

Professor Michael Wright

Professor Michael Wright is the Vice Chancellor of Canterbury Christ Church University and, from 1997, was the Principal in its earlier position as a College and University College. His academic discipline is law. Before Canterbury, he taught law and was an academic manager at universities in Bristol, Glasgow and Edinburgh. Both personally and in a professional capacity he has been a member of a number of

education, church and community organisations. He is a Lay
Canon of Canterbury Cathedral and a Deputy Lieutenant of
the County of Kent. He is a former Chairman of the Council
of Church Universities and Colleges (Britain) and chairs the
Board of Trustees of the Colleges and Universities of the
Anglican Communion.

Dr Joel Cunningham

Joel Cunningham has been Vice Chancellor, President, and
Professor of Mathematics at Sewanee: The University of the
South since 2000. From 1979 to 2000 he was a faculty member
and administrator at Susquehanna University, first as Vice
President for Academic Affairs and Professor of Mathematics and, from 1984, as President. An early member of the
Campus Compact for student public service and a trustee of
the Council of Independent Colleges, Cunningham chaired
the Commission on Policy Analysis of the National Association of Independent Colleges and Universities and was president of the Society for Values in Higher Education. He has
been Chair of the Association of Episcopal Colleges, the
Appalachian College Association, and the Tennessee Independent Colleges and Universities Association; and Treasurer of the Colleges and Universities of the Anglican
Communion. He has served as a leader in the Lilly Endow-
ment-funded Council of Independent Colleges program on
vocation and mission for college presidents and prospective
presidents and is one of the founders of the Vocation
in Undergraduate Education initiative.

Dr Nirmala Jeyaraj

Dr. Nirmala Jeyaraj, MSc, PhD is the former Program director (2008–09)of the United Board for Christian Higher Education (UBCHEA), Hong Kong and former Principal (1996–2008) of Lady Doak College, Madurai, India. She is a Biologist specialized in Molecular Biology and has more than three decades of teaching and research experience with several publications to her credit. She was a Visiting Professor for a year at St. Andrew's Presbyterian College, North Carolina, USA and a Visiting Scholar at the Wolffson Institute of Biotechnology, University of Sheffield, UK. Based on her exposure and experience in Higher Education in both Asia and the West, she has published several articles on various issues in Higher Education and has edited books on the same. She has also held other leadership positions such as the Vice President of All India Association for Christian Higher Education (AIACHE), Member and Chair of the Executive Committee of CUAC and a member of the Syndicate of Madurai Kamaraj University.

Reverend Dr Jeremy Law

Jeremy Law is currently Dean of Chapel at Canterbury Christ Church University, a position he has held since 2003. After a geology degree at Aberystwyth and postgraduate research in geology at Leeds University, Jeremy trained for the Church of England ministry at Salisbury and Wells Theological College. As part of his training he completed a theology degree via Southampton University. Ordained in 1987, he followed a Curacy at Wimborne Minster in Dorset with an Oxford

DPhil in the theology of Jürgen Moltmann under the supervision of Rowan Williams and Paul Fiddes. For nine years, from 1994, he was Lazenby Chaplain and Lecturer in Theology at Exeter University. His research interests and recent publications have included work on the theology of human evolution, the ecological interpretation of theology and a theology of boundary that seeks to link together the being of God and the origin of life.

Professor Gerald J Pillay

Gerald John Pillay was born in the former British colony of Natal in South Africa. He was awarded a BA, a BD (with distinction) and Doctor of Theology from the University of Durban. He also achieved a DPhil in Philosophical Theology from Rhodes University.

After lecturing at the University of Durban-Westville he became Professor of Ecclesiastical History at the University of South Africa in 1988, a post he held for eight years. During this period he was also variously Guest Professor at North Western University, Illinois; Research Fellow at Princeton University; Visiting Professor at Eastern Mennonite University, Virginia; Guest Professor at Rhodes University and Visiting Professor at the graduate school at AMBS, Indiana.

In 1997 he became Foundation Professor and Head of the Department of Theology and Religious Studies at Otago University, New Zealand's oldest University, based in Dunedin in the South Island. He was asked to serve as the first Head of Liberal Arts within that University in 1998. He has served in various senior leadership roles at the University of South

Africa, the Human Sciences Research Council in Pretoria and the University of Otago.

In 2003 he was appointed head of Liverpool Hope University College—an institution whose first founding College was established in 1844. He became its first Vice-Chancellor when Liverpool Hope was given full university status in July 2005.

Professor Pillay has served on editorial boards of two international journals (*Studia Historiae Ecclesiasticae and Verbum et Ecclesia*), has presented papers at numerous international conferences and has served on various public and educational bodies. He has published extensively and is an internationally respected scholar.

A New Zealand citizen, Professor Pillay is a Deputy Lieutenant of the County of Merseyside.

Dame Janet Trotter

Dame Janet Trotter trained to teach religious studies at a Church College in the 1960s and taught a range of secondary school pupils for eight years before joining King Alfred's College Winchester as a lecturer in Theology and Education. In 1978 she was promoted to the position of Head of Professional Education. From there she was seconded to Church House Westminster in 1984 to be interim College's Officer during a period of transition for all voluntary colleges in the UK and then moved to Lancaster to be Vice Principal of St Martin's College.

In 1986 she became Principal of the College of St. Paul and St. Mary in Cheltenham and led it through merger to university title in 2001. She had a number of national roles while in this position and was a member of the Higher Education Funding Council, the Teacher Training Agency and the Quality Assurance Agency (Degree Awarding Powers Advisory Committee).

Dame Janet retired from the University of Gloucester in 2006. She currently chairs the Foundation for Church Leadership, the Gloucestershire Hospitals Foundation Trust and Winston's Wish, a charity for bereaved children: she is also a member of the governing bodies of two universities.

Dame Janet has honorary degrees from a number of universities, both in the UK and overseas, and was made a Dame Commander of the British Empire in 2001.

Contents

Introduction

The origins of this book, which can perhaps best be described as a collection of personal essays in which the contributors reflect upon their experience, lie in various conversations which the editors have had during the past ten years. Each of us has spent time over those years considering, from both a practical and theoretical perspective, what it means to have leadership responsibilities in Christian higher education.

- Is it different to higher education generally?
- How does it extend beyond 'signs and symbols'?
- How has the challenge changed over the years?
- Are there any lessons to be learned from taking an international perspective?
- Are there differences between the various Christian denominations?
- What is the role of chaplaincy?
- How and in what ways should the curriculum reflect a Christian dimension?

This collection of essays does not purport to offer the answers to those questions although it does touch on all of them. What it does do is to offer the considered views of a number of people with whom we have worked over the years and whose reflections would, in our opinion, be of interest and assistance to those facing the challenge of leadership in Christian higher education. The essay have not been edited other than for the purpose of producing a consistent style.

We are grateful to the Archbishop of Canterbury, the Chancellor of Canterbury Christ Church University, for his contribution which, at his request, he prepared once he had had the opportunity of reading all the essays.

The book in no sense represents an attempt to offer a prescription for effective leadership of a Christian university. It is simply intended to stimulate further reflection and discussion on a matter which we regard as both important and interesting. We hope it achieves that objective.

Professor Michael Wright
Professor James Arthur

Canterbury, December 2009

James Arthur

Greater Expectations

Vision and Leadership in Christian Higher Education

The very essence of leadership is that you have to have a vision. It's got to be a vision you articulate clearly and forcefully on every occasion.

Theodore Hesburgh,
President of the University of Notre Dame

In 1867 the noted agnostic John Stuart Mill gave a three hour inaugural address on his election to the honorary position of Rector of St. Andrew's University in Scotland. He described what he thought should guide a university and was insistent that 'it is a very imperfect education which trains the intellect only, but not the will ... The moral or religious influence which a university can exercise, consists less in any express teaching, than in the pervading tone of the place ... It should present all knowledge as chiefly a means to worthiness of life.' Mill believed that this would be done by personal influence, as he said: 'There is nothing which spreads more contagiously from teacher to pupil than elevation of sentiment'. In an age prior to the secularisation of the universities Mill still thought, as a secularist, that religion of some kind could form part of the purpose of an university education and he even regretted that 'the great question of the relation of education to religion' was suffering from the dogmatism of the religious on one hand and the secularists on the other (see Robson, 1984: 348). John Henry Newman, writing his *Idea of a University* a couple of decades before had of course insisted that the tone of a university and the personal influence exercised by its leaders were essential ingredients of providing for a liberal education.

In an early sermon of 1832, 'Personal Influence, the Means of Propagating the Truth,' Newman asks how Christianity has made its way and held its ground in the world. He answers that its chief strength has not been in rational arguments, but rather it has 'been upheld in the world not as a system, not by books, not by arguments, nor by temporal power, but by the personal influence...'. It is impossible to understand Newman without grasping the depth of his commitment to the principle of 'personal influence' which pervades all his writings. Personal influence, for Newman was more important than organisation and books, as he said: 'The heart is commonly reached, not through reason, but through the imagination, by means of direct impressions, by the testimony of facts and events, by history, by description. Persons influence us, voices melt us, looks subdue us, deeds inflame us'. You could say he had a theory of 'personal influence' born out of his own life and practice and he emphasized constantly the importance of imbuing the whole secular order with a Christian spirit and tone—including education. For Newman, the 'personal presence of a teacher' was indispensable for education of any kind and he therefore adopted what might be called a 'personalist' approach to education. In regard to leadership in higher education it could be said that the purpose is to influence others and to enthusiastically pursue identifiable goals related to the core mission of an institution.

In a recent lecture Alasdair MacIntyre (2009) described how Newman gives two more or less complementary accounts of the meaning of the word 'university': the first being viewed from the aspect of what is taught there, the second from the aspect of those who constitute it and what they do. Newman therefore complements the essence of the University with the need for a higher principle of authority as its guide and governor, which he defines as its *integrity*. Newman's own words from 'The Rise and Progress of Universities' on the power of knowledge that is personally embodied is pertinent here:

> I say then, that the personal influence of the teacher is able in some sort to dispense with an academical system, but that the system cannot in any sort dispense with personal influence. With influence there is life, without it there is none; if influence is deprived of its due position, it will not by those means be got rid of, it will only break out irregularly, dangerously. An academical system without the personal influence of teachers upon pupils is an arctic winter; it will create an ice-bound, petrified, cast-iron University, and nothing else.

The personal influence of a leader of a Christian University is the key to the kind of tone established and the direction given to that higher education institution. The first duty of a leader in a Christian institution is to be always willingly identified as a Christian by students and staff and by all who visit the College or University. Church affiliation does not make a university Christian, but the ethos created and sustained through personal leadership can make the difference in these institutions.

The Christian faith must surely inform the leader of a Christian institution to what values are worthwhile and so leadership must be therefore a process of personal influence that emphasizes goals—quite simply it is leadership as a result of what one believes, values and does. Indeed, the power in the vision for an institution is not usually captured by its mission statement, but it certainly can by its leader on the basis of their vision and principles, producing a leadership that is underpinned by the motivations and passion behind their actions, thoughts and words. There are two immediate challenges to this personal influence and tone setting. First, some might argue that Christianity seldom dictates leadership that is distinctive in the sense that non-Christians might not say or do more or less the same thing on a given subject. Second, it is also not clear that particular Christian commitments produce or lead to leadership styles which set Christians apart from everyone else. Therefore, there does not seem to be any specifically 'Christian' view on leadership, just as there is correspondingly no such thing as a stereotypical Christian higher education institution. Christian higher education institutions can and do differ dramatically from each other and it is important to recognize that there is no single way to understand and implement their stated vision. Nevertheless, the values of an institution should be observable in the leadership as well as in the environment. Consequently, all leaders of Christian institutions should be asking some common questions that have a direct relationship to their faith and chief among these is: How should their Christian faith relate to their leadership? George Marsden, a Protestant, accepted a teaching position at Notre Dame University because he wanted to be part of a 'school where religious questions were more central to the intellectual life of the institution'. Surely all universities with a Christian heritage must be places where religious questions are debated within the mainstream of intellectual life? In addition, leadership within the Christian sector of higher education faces a more thoroughly secularized society than did Mill or Newman and so it is perhaps first necessary to understand the origins of the kind of society and mind set of the modern student and lecturer.

There are many higher education colleges and universities that were founded under the auspices of a Church and which are now not legally connected to any denomination: their status as a church institution being essentially historical. Accordingly, most universities once had religious seals such as Harvard University, which had a seal *In Christi gloriam* in the seventeenth century, but which was changed to *Pro Christo et Ecclesiae* (for Christ and the Church) in the late eighteenth century. This was changed again in 1884 to *Veritas* to reflect its more secular orientation as a modern research university. Advocates of secular education were uncomfortable and perhaps even embarrassed by the religious origins of universities. The majority of what are now called 'secular' universities in the UK followed this same pattern in the late nineteenth and early twentieth centuries. However, in the changing of Harvard's seal it did not become more of a university, but simply a different sort of university. It seems that if you want to be a 'real' university there is pressure on you to abandon all sense of denominational commitment. Many of the Anglican colleges that have become universities in recent years within England choose to name themselves after a City, rather than to retain their original names which often gave some indication of their religious heritage. They have also committed themselves to a series of 'values' often as a way of affirming some kind of continuity with their religious heritage, but by stressing 'values' they are often saying almost nothing and in fact actually may be contributing to their loss of religious identity. We therefore need to ask some deep questions about contemporary Anglican higher education. Are Christian affiliated colleges 'university' enough to satisfy the academic establishment, or alternatively are they religious enough to satisfy the religious community that founded them? Or is there a rhetorical rather than a real commitment to the Christian foundation of these universities? After all, religious origins do not presuppose current commitment.

'Christian higher education' is taken here to refer to education in Higher Education Institutions where Christianity is privileged at an institutional level, both in their legal documents and in at least some of their official ceremonies. A stronger definition would be those universities or colleges

that use their Christian vision or identity as one of the organizing paradigms (Benne 2001).A Christian affiliated university in England today serves the broader society of which it is
part and it certainly has wider obligations to the whole of
society. It requires high levels of expenditure and is subject to
a whole range of increasing demands, not least from government legislation and external pressures from many sources.
In an earlier era, the Christian mission of these colleges was
simply presumed, seemingly guaranteed by the force of their
history and the background of there students and staff.
However, new circumstances have arisen and the religious
distinctiveness of these institutions is no longer readily
apparent. There is genuine concern that some Christian universities and colleges have pursued a secular model to such
an extent that their identity and mission within the Church is
no longer clear or shared. Whilst Newman's goals for a
Christian University regularly receive numerous tributes
and ritualistic praise from Vice Chancellors and Principals in
speeches, his influence on policy and planning in Christian
higher education has been minimal. Instead, what we see is
an academic leadership that too often subscribes to the safe
course of allowing political expediency dictate mission and
policy which has resulted in a secularization that is erasing
their *raison d' etre*. The leadership of Christian affiliated colleges and universities are all acutely aware of the difficulties,
but this raises the question as to whether the Christian
dimension of these institutions is gravely ill or even termi-
nally so? Can the Church community that founded these
institutions be optimistic about their future? Can something
religiously worthwhile be salvaged?

There is undoubtedly a clash between worldviews in academia that presuppose God and those that do not. Charles Taylor (2008: 2) notes that we have moved from a society where belief in God is unchallenged and unproblematic to one in which it is merely one option among many others. Stanley Hauerwas (2007: 173) has further observed that 'the habits that constitutes the secular imagination are so embedded in how Christian's understand the world we no longer have the ability to recognise the power they have over us'. Modern secular currents of thought function to undercut religious belief and practice and indeed make it hard to sustain faith and belief among contemporary Christians. Nevertheless, a secular world or society is not necessarily a society without God, but it is a society without a religion in the public spaces and that includes the public spaces that are our universities. Moreover, an exclusive naturalist worldview of promoting certain values that are almost indistinguishable in practice from Christian values may lead to a soft or mild kind of secularism – the first stage in moving towards full blowing secularism. For example, the virtues of care and compassion are encouraged in the secular professions, but not because we are commanded by God to love our neighbour. The difference in the operation of these values lies in the intentions, motivations and sense of priorities that people have and display. Whilst Christian higher education institutions today are certainly pluralist by their very nature, with competing and contrasting values, it still remains for the leader to focus on the foundation values, to promulgate a vision and nurture a Christian culture within the institution. The Principal has care of the mission of the institution and should be unafraid to talk about it and celebrate it. In brief, they should speak with a relevant voice to the secularity of society. Do they have something distinctive to contribute to society? Indeed, do, or should, our Christian affiliated universities function differently in the preparation and formation of teachers, nurses, community workers, social workers, and police officers?

The dominant contemporary worldview in higher education is underpinned by a secular ideology of education. The ideal of neutrality for secular education is something that is advocated at a philosophical level by educationalists who wish to see a neutral learning framework or a philosophy of education that is neutral about a student's ultimate beliefs. Theoretically secularists seek neutrality between varied religious and non-religious worldviews—an education, they claim, that neither promotes nor inhibits religion. Education has certainly become narrowly identified by secular educational philosophers with rationality and the concepts 'secular' and 'rational' have been equated. MacIntyre (1988 and 1990) has argued that it is false to insist that there is just one thing called 'rationality'. He instead proposes that there are in fact different 'traditions' of rationality such as the Aristotelian, Augustinian, Scottish Common-Sense versions and others. Each is a different intellectual culture and each can sustain wide intellectual debate, but all of which argue from different assumptions. Rationality, for MacIntyre, means consistency or coherence within one or another of these traditions. Therefore, at least one of these traditions of rationality may be viewed as religious which he insists is no disqualification.

The danger in Christian institutions is that they adopt the secular approach of claiming to respect all religious views by ignoring them in practice. The assumption made is that religious arguments are more divisive and sectarian than secular arguments and should thus be bracketed out of public discussion. This makes the mistake of failing to acknowledge the power of faith in people's lives. It results in the avoidance of discussing religion for fear of offending anyone. Secular institutions and governments are not neutral in their effects between different ways of life as they undermine some and promote others. The presuppositions of such secular agencies are inescapably hostile to Christianity. Do our Vice Chancellors and Principals value the importance of a Christian academic vision in the life of their institutions? Do they ensure that a Christian account is heard or do they shut out such visions from academic discussions? What tradition of rationality is operative in their institutions? Is it the understanding of truth that MacIntyre (2009b: 68–69) speaks of in *God, Philosophy and Universities*?

> First, the attainment of truth is integral to the goal of understanding. Acts of understanding always involve knowledge of truths and of the relationship of those truths to others. Second, insofar as the achievement of a perfected understanding of the nature of things requires relating the truths of theology to those of a variety of other disciplines, it matters not only that within each discipline enquirers acknowledge the various standards by which truth is discriminated from falsity, but also that they share a single concept of truth that gives point and purpose

to the application of those standards. Third and finally, the project of understanding is not one only for those engaged in teaching, studying, and enquiring within universities. Every one of us, in our everyday lives, needs in a variety of ways to learn and to understand. The ability of those outside universities to learn and to understand what they need to learn can be helped or hindered by the good or bad effects on their intellectual formation and their thinking of those who have been educated in universities, by the good or bad influence, that is not only of parents, but also of school teachers, pastors, and others. One condition for that influence being good rather than bad is that what is communicated to and shared by the whole community of teachers and learners is a respect for truth and a grasp of truths that presupposes, ... an adequate conception of truth.

The aims of secular education have become premised on the belief that there is nothing beyond the natural, the physical world—no soul, no mystery and no supernatural. Ultimate values exclusively reside in human beings and possess no supernatural origins. If something appears to exist or lay beyond the natural world then this is simply something that is imperfectly understood in the present – it will, the argument goes, eventually be understood and fall within the natural. Religious beliefs and practices are accordingly considered nothing more than natural phenomenon to be accounted for by human causes. The aims of learning in this account become understood within a framework of pragmaticism and rationality with students taught to interpret the world in terms of human outcomes and results—a scientific explanation of the world. The purpose of secular education is consequently intended to socialise students into a powerful set of naturalistic political assumptions, affections and practices. It uncritically initiates students into secular ways of thinking by using secular categories of explanation that exclude or ignore alternatives. In particular, it deliberately ignores religious ways of thinking about the world. It functions to undercut religious loyalties and advances non-theistic belief systems. Secular education is informed by an ideology that privileges impersonal, deterministic forces at the expense of moral agency. If Christian affiliated institutions operate such a system of education then the tone and personal influence exercised in them will be wholly secular. This unofficial naturalism in the university becomes unable to justify a distinction between human and all other life-forms and yet professional education courses, which attract the vast majority of students in Christian affiliated higher education institutions, always relate to a view of the human. Leaders of Christian affiliated colleges and universities must ask themselves whether the Christian account is still publicly relevant in the educational life of the institution. Also, why is it that many staff and students are not aware of any religious connection?

It is not therefore surprising that the leadership of Christian higher education institutions is often beset with ambiguities. In England there are 15 remaining Christian affiliated colleges and universities. In the 1950s Christian perspectives on higher education retained a significant presence in public debate and in some academic discussions, whatever the decline in private belief and practice. Moberly's *The Crisis of the University* published in 1949, resisted the notion of a 'Christian University' on the grounds that insights from Christianity already reinforced the 'basis of values and virtues' which ought to characterise every university's intellectual endeavour, but he recognised that external forces represented the greatest threat to this tradition. Government legislation has certainly been one of the greatest threats, especially as such legislation on the governance and funding of higher education has been extensive. It is in a way inevitable that in a system of higher education that depends almost entirely on central government for funding for its core activities of research and teaching that the government will increasingly determine the aims and practices of higher education itself. The Christian affiliated colleges and universities in England that have expanded were even more dependent on government-funded courses and many of them closed between 1970 and 2001 — falling from 54 to 15. These colleges and universities are open to all students and in no way discriminate on the basis of religious affiliation for admission. They are effectively public universities serving the common good, but retain a legitimate and important distinctive religious heritage. Unfortunately, those that continue to hold and keep alive this heritage are often isolated individuals within the wider university culture with their voices being lost or difficult to hear. It is the leader's responsibility to ensure that these voices from the sponsoring heritage are concerted and have a central place in the institution's life. Indeed, you could say that heads of a Christian higher education institution have a duty to bring together academics concerned with faith and learning.

In England, it could be argued, that the transformation of some colleges into universities affiliated to the Church of England, has resulted in them becoming largely secular institutions where religion has been disestablished from its defining role by a long and relentless secularisation process. This process has not been started by some dramatic decision of the Principal or Governors, but through erosion. As James Nuechterlein (1993: 16) says:

> The movement from religious commitment to secularity was the result most often not of any secularist plot but rather of a fit of absence of mind …The critical steps down the slippery slope to secularity were almost always initiated by administrators and faculty members who did not intend secularity at all … Almost all of the formerly Christian institutions that capitulated to secularity lost their religious identity incrementally and by inadvertence, not by one critical step or conscious policy.

Christianity has become one perspective among many in the academic strategy for organising the curriculum, and the main thrust of these institutions has become the practical educational task of equipping students with skills to find jobs. Academic departments rarely relate their objectives to the Christian mission of the institution. However, some of these institutions continue to respect their relationship with the Church of England, and there is still some representation of the vision and ethos of the Anglican tradition in the college or university's life and governance. Most of these institutions have an Anglican majority on the governing body. It could be said that they retain a unique and rather complex set of governance arrangements which are a result of their religious mission and foundation. The Christian presence is still guaranteed in the form of ensuring the appointment of senior management who retain an Anglican connection, particularly in the appointment of the Principal and chaplain who usually must be communicant members of the Church of England.

However, this strategy is accommodated within a fundamentally secular model for defining the identity and mission of the university. The Anglican connection neither dominates or disappears, but sufficient numbers of academics must continue to be convinced that the representation of Anglicanism is a good thing. However, since a growing majority of staff and students in this understanding are not part of the sponsoring tradition, it may become a difficult to maintain even the most modest representation of the heritage. The real danger is that they simply become 'shadowy imitations of secular institutions' and imitate the worst features of secular higher education. In the *Closing of the American Mind* Allan Bloom described the problem of the modern university this way 'The University now offers no distinctive visage to the young person ... there is no vision, nor is there a set of competing visions, of what an educated human being is'. There is certainly a vagueness of the language of mission statements and the indeterminacy of their acknowledged commitments. They often frame their mission in such a way that they seriously lack anything specifically Christian. It is usually easier and certainly less risky to do nothing than to

attempt change. Maxims of these institutions speak of a former religious intensity now long since dead, but once a
Christian identity has gone is it irretrievable? Many leaders
of Christian institutions simply do not feel equipped to make
a difference to their colleges or universities in any specifically
Christian way—always asking what is permissible, what is
legal or what is appropriate. In the end the greatest contribution they could make to pluralism in society is not pretend
that pluralism makes no difference—but rather that they
insist that higher education in a Christian institution is a different kind of university.

Respecting the religious viewpoints of students and
lecturers, rather than simply fending them off, could enrich
academic debates. A Christian affiliated university should be
a place where Christians find a conducive environment to do
their thinking. It needs committed people who understand
and can articulate a clear vision. Fewer people are identified
with the sponsoring tradition and as they decline the influence of the sponsoring tradition declines with them. Clearly
no Christian affiliated college or university today is Christian
in the pervasive way that many once were. Nevertheless, few
of them are completely secularised either. The essential element that makes all the difference is what Benne (2001: 96)
concludes is without faithful persons from a thriving tradition who bear the vision and ethos of that tradition, a college
or university will lose its identity.

Robert Benne (2001) in his excellent book, *Quality with
Soul*, informs us that many Christian affiliated colleges and
universities find themselves somewhere between the poles
of 'fully Christian' on one side and complete secularization

on the other. He provides a detailed typology of Christian affiliated institutions on a continuum from maximal to minimal connection of colleges and universities and their religious heritage He effectively classifies institutions according to the extent of their commitment to their religious heritage. The two categories that best describe Christian affiliated higher education institutions in Britain are on the minimum end of the continuum: the 'intentionally pluralist' and 'accidentally pluralist'. In these two types of institutions the Christian perspective is not normative, but rather must make its way among the many different viewpoints on offer In summary, Benne (2001:51) explains that:

> The intentionally pluralist college or university respects its relation to its sponsoring heritage enough that it intentionally places members of that heritage in important positions, starting with the president. There is a straightforward or tacit commitment to representation of the vision and ethos of the tradition here and there is the [institution's] life …This strategy is accommodated within a fundamentally secular model for defining the identity and mission of the college …Christian presence, through very much disestablished, is nevertheless guaranteed in some form.

In contrast, the 'accidentally pluralist' model fails to commit itself to the sponsoring tradition and does not operate the institution out of a religious vision, rather the institution leaves Christian representation among the staff and students largely to chance. Benne suggests that we ought to find ways to strengthen the partial connections they have to their sponsoring tradition and even find new connections. However, he recognizes that such a strategy for re-connection has a certain level of fragility about it. A leadership of setting the tone and employing personal influence within the institution is of course key to any re-connection, but a certain kind of leadership can also disconnect the institution even further from its religious heritage. It is questionable whether such a university can begin and continue to be staffed with enough Christians.

It is widely acknowledge that chapel services attract only a very small number of students and staff in most Christian affiliated colleges and universities, but what happens to the chapel and chaplain is normally a good indicator of how seriously the Christian account is taken by the leadership. Take for example the appointment of chaplains. Are the chaplain(s) from the sponsoring tradition or one among a number of options? Do they conduct services in the chapel according to a regular schedule or do they only conduct services on special occasions which are intended to be strictly 'inclusive'? Is the chapel used exclusively for worship or used for other educational purposes? Is the chaplain full-time or part-time? Is the chapel peripheral to the life of the college or university? All of these questions raise serious questions about whether a leader wishes to re-connect with the religious heritage of the institution. Chaplains are not normally members of the senior management team, but there is a case that they ought to be of such a caliber to influence the direction of the Christian university or college through theological thinking. The danger is that the chaplain becomes entirely focused on student welfare and chapel services for a small minority. Similar questions can be asked of theology departments—are the courses they run mainly in other traditions and religions than in the specific tradition that sponsors the institution? Is the study of theology, and of religion more generally prioritized? Are Christian world-views explored and articulated? Is research facilitated in areas that complement a Christian worldview? Is learning and teaching underpinned by some dimensions of a Christian worldview which affects what is studied and how it is studied? Such questioning can extend out to other departments and to the life in the university or college as a whole to judge whether it has a pervasively secular tone or not.

The Church of England working group called *Mutual Expectations* looked at the expectations of Anglican institutes of higher education and reported in 2005. The working group examined the distinctiveness of Anglican higher education and Nicholas Sagovsky (2009: 1–7), a member of the group, recommended that it 'go back to theological first principles' in order to understand what it means to be a 'Christian institution' and the way in which Christian principles and values might inform the life of such an educational institution. His conclusion was that an Anglican university turns on a certain understanding of the incarnation. However, this strong theological aim for Anglican institutions did not find its way into the final report. An earlier Church report called *The Way Ahead* reported in 2001 (2001: 70) concluded that: 'We consider it essential that all those appointed to senior positions in the colleges should be in sympathy with, and willing and able to support, the mission of the colleges as Christian institutions' and 'We would go further and so we recommend to the colleges that as a long term policy, the head of the teacher training should be a practicing Christian'. Both reports emphasised the importance of the tone or ethos of Christian higher education together with the leadership qualities of the principals. However, questions need to be asked of the Churches themselves as they are not always clear about what they really expect from their higher education institutions. The Church of England continues to talk of partnership, but is there still one? Does the Church understand government policy on higher education?

The Colleges and Universities of the Anglican Communion (CUAC) was formed as a world-wide association of Anglican colleges and universities of higher education as a result of an International Conference of representatives assembled at Canterbury in 1993 (Christ Church College, UK), in order to examine issues of values within the context of church-related higher education. The CUAC founded a refereed journal, called *Prologue*, that focused on the issues, trends, opportunities, and challenges of international Anglican higher education. The mission and purpose of *Prologue* was described as follows:

> Founded in 1993, the Colleges and Universities of the Anglican Communion is a worldwide association of over 100 institutions of higher education network that were founded by or retain ties to a branch of the Anglican Communion. With contributors and readers on five continents, *Prologue* offers diverse perspectives on the unique mission of church related colleges and universities throughout the world.

In January, 2009 the Trustees of the Colleges and Universities of the Anglican Communion decided to suspend publication of the journal *Prologue*. This decision does not necessarily advance the aims of the association.

The problem that leaders of Christian higher education institutions often struggle with is how to be part of the mainstream of academia without sacrificing specifically Christian contributions that are both unique and valuable to society. As Richard Neuhaus asks (1996) 'The question that those who lead a Christian university must answer, and answer again every day, is whether the confession that Jesus is Lord limits or illumines the university's obligation to seek and serve (*Veritas*) — to seek and serve the truth.' The lack of a general theological awareness among many who lead these institutions can result in a reductionist ethos. Christian leaders need to ensure that their institutions have a curriculum that offers Christian insights and values, research that advances the declared Christian purpose of the institution, and a significant proportion of staff and students who make up the community who are willing and able to contribute to its values and mission. Otherwise the core of the institution's identity could be defined by external secular agencies and government. Leaders of Christian higher education institutions need to directly and publicly acknowledge their Christian dimension. They should renounce the kind of conscious or unconscious ambiguity in their leadership that seeks to have it both ways: a touch of religion for the Christian constituency, but basic secularity for the non-Christian. Within the context of such a forthright commitment, their college or university would be open to students of all religions or none, to interfaith relationships and to freedom for academic exploration and inquiry. There is a positive generosity about the Christian tradition which ought to generate a new confidence amongst universities at large and which we need. We need to ask how Christian leadership will regain confidence and cease to be regarded as defending a lost cause? The answer is to focus on God and the resources of the Christian tradition.

In conclusion, universities and colleges that merely recognize a historic connection to a church or denomination or whose identity or affiliation does not influence their mission downplay Christian distinctiveness in order to accommodate pluralism. Thus, while many of these institutions may mention the goal of spiritual or ethical development, this development is disconnected from the Christian identity of the institution. The questions leaders must honestly answer are: Does the institution acknowledge their Christian or confessional identity in their mission statement as more than a piece of history? Is the Christian identity mentioned in the marketing to students? Does the Principal or Vice-Chancellor acknowledge the Christian identity in his or her web page and in welcoming students? Does the institution see itself as first and foremost as a national or regional institution and not as a Christian institution?

Those leaders who are open to ways of pursuing Christian agendas and perspectives in higher education, but want to see some models of how to proceed have an excellent range of authors to consult. As well as the references made in this text to various authors every Principal of a Christian affiliated college or university should also have the following texts on their shelves and in their libraries: George M Marsden's *The Soul of the American University* and *The Outrageous*

Idea of Christian Scholarship, Jaroslav Pelikan's *The Idea of the University*, Douglas Sloan's *Faith and Knowledge*, Theodore Hesburgh's *The Challenge and Promise of the University*, James Burchaell's *The Decline and Fall of the Christian College*, James W Sire's *Habits of the Mind*, Mark A Noll's *The Scandal of the Evangelical Mind* and Alasdair MacIntyre's *God, Philosophy and Universities*. I have also included a select bibliography on Christian higher education at the end of the references.

References

Audi, Robert (2005), Moral Foundations of liberal Democracy, Secular Reasons, and liberal Neutrality Towards the Good', *Notre Dame Journal of Law, Ethics and Public Policy*, 19:197–218.

Benne, R. (2001), *Quality with Soul: How Six Premier Colleges and Universities Keep Faith With Their Religious Traditions*, Grand Rapids, MI: Eerdmans.

Budde, M. and Wright, J. (eds.) (2004), *Conflicting Allegiances*, Grand Rapids, MI: Brazos Press.

Casanova, J. (1994), *Public Religion in the Modern World*, Chicago: Chicago University Press.

Hauerwas, S. (2007), *The State of the University*, Oxford: Blackwell.

MacIntyre, A. (2009), The Very Idea of a University: Aristotle, Newman and US, *British Journal of Educational Studies*, Vol. 57 No. 4.

MacIntyre, A. (2009b), *God, Philosophy, Universities: A Selective History of the Catholic Philosophical Tradition*, New York: Rowman and Littlefield.

Mill, J. S. (1984), Essays on equality, Law and Education, *Collected Works of John Stuart Mill*, Vol. XXI edited by J. Robson, Toronto: Toronto University Press.

Neuhaus, R. J. (1996), The Christian University: Eleven Theses, *First Things* (January).

Nuechterlein, J. (1993) The Idol of Academic Freedom, *First Things* (December).

Taylor, C. (2007) *The Secular Age*, Cambridge: Harvard University Press.

Recommended Select Bibliography on Christian Higher Education

Catholic

Buckley, M. J. (1998) *The Catholic University as Promise and Project*, Washington, DC: Georgetown University Press.

Gleason, P. (1995), *Contending with Modernity: Catholic Higher Education in the Twentieth Century*, New York, NY: Oxford University Press.

John Paul II (1990), *On Catholic Universities: Ex corde ecclesiae*, London: Catholic Truth Society.

Mahoney, K. A. (2003), *Catholic Higher Education in Protestant America*, Baltimore, MD: Johns Hopkins University Press.

Morey, M. M. and Piderit, J. J. (2006), *Catholic Higher Education: A Culture in Crisis*, New York, NY: Oxford University Press.

O'Brien, G. D. (2002) *The Idea of a Catholic University*, Chicago, IL: University of Chicago Press.

Roche, M. W. (2003), *The Intellectual Appeal of Catholicism & the Idea of a Catholic University*, Notre Dame, IN: University of Notre Dame.

For additional works on Catholic Higher Education see the bibliography by Thomas M. Landy and Paula Powell Sapienza http://www.collegium.org/reading.html

Christian Higher Education – General

Benne, R. (2001), *Quality with Soul: How Six Premier Colleges and Universities Keep Faith With Their Religious Traditions*, Grand Rapids, MI: Eerdmans.

Budde, M. and Wright, J. (eds.) (2004), *Conflicting Allegiances: The Church-Based University in a Liberal Democratic Society*, Grand Rapids, MI: Brazos.

Cuninggim, M. (1994), *Uneasy Partners: The college and the Church*, Nashville, TN: Abingdon Press.

D'Costa, G. (2005) *Theology in the public square: Church, academy and nation*, Malden, MA: Blackwell Publishing.

Diekema, A. J. (2000), *Academic Freedom and Christian Scholarship*, Grand Rapids, MI: William B. Eerdmans Publishing Company.

Dockery, D. S. and Thornbury, G. A. (2002), *Shaping a Christian Worldview: Foundations of Christian Higher Education*, Nashville: Broadman and Holman Publishers.

Dovre, P. J. (ed.) (2002), *The Future of Religious Colleges*, Grand Rapids, MI: Eerdmans.

Hughes, R. T. and Adrian, W. B. (eds.) (1997), *Models for Christian Higher Education: Strategies for Success in the Twenty-First Century*, Grand Rapids, MI: Eerdmans.

Jacobsen, D. G. and Jacobsen, R. H. (eds) (2004), *Scholarship and Christian Faith: Enlarging the Conversation*, New York, NY: Oxford University Press.

Litfin, D. (2004), *Conceiving the Christian college*, Grand Rapids, MI: William B. Eerdmans Publishing Company.

Marsden, G. M. (1997), *The Outrageous Idea of Christian Scholarship*, New York, NY: Oxford University Press.

MacIntyre, A. (2009), *God, Philosophy, Universities: A Selective History of the Catholic Philosophical Tradition*, New York, Rowman and Littlefield.

Mannoia, V. J., Jr. (2000), *Christian Liberal Arts*, Lanham, MD: Rowman and Littlefield.

Migliazzo, A. C. (ed.) (2002), *Teaching as an Act of Faith: Theory and Practice in Church-Related Higher Education*, New York, NY: Fordham University Press.

Noll, M. A. (1994), *The Scandal of the Evangelical Mind*, Grand Rapids, MI: William B. Eerdmans Publishing Company.

Poe, H. L. (2004), *Christianity in the Academy: Teaching at the Intersection of Faith and Learning*, Grand Rapids, MI: Baker Academic.

Ringenberg, W. (2006), *The Christian College: A History of Protestant Higher Education in America*, Grand Rapids, MI: Baker Academic.

Roberts, J., and Turner, J. (2000), *The sacred and the secular university*, Princeton, NJ: Princeton University Press.

Schaffer Riley, N. (2005), *God on the Quad: How Religious Colleges and the Missionary Generation Are Changing America*, New York, NY: St. Martin's.

Schwehn, M. R. (1993), *Exiles from Eden: Religion and the Academic Vocation in America*, New York, NY: Oxford University Press.

Simon, C. J. *et al.* (2003), *Mentoring for Mission: Nurturing New Faculty at Church-Related Colleges*, Grand Rapids, MI: William B. Eerdmans Publishing Company.

Sterk, A. (ed.) (2002), *Religion, Scholarship and Higher Education: Perspectives, Models and Future Prospects: Essays from the Lilly Seminar on Religion and Higher Education*, Notre Dame, IN: University of Notre Dame Press.

Thiessen, E. J. (2001), *In Defence of Religious Schools and Colleges*, Montreal, Quebec: McGill-Queen's University Press.

Turner, J. (2003), *Language, Religion, Knowledge: Past and Present*, Notre Dame, IN: University of Notre Dame Press.

Wolterstorff, N., Joldersma, C. W. and Stronks, G. (eds.) (2002), *Educating for Shalom: Essays on Christian Higher Education*, Grand Rapids, MI: Eerdmans.

Christian Higher Education – History

Burtchaell, J. T. (1998) *The Dying of the Light: The Disengagement of the Colleges and Universities from their Christian Churches*, Grand Rapids, MI: Eerdmans.

Marsden, G. M. (1994), *The Soul of the American University: From Protestant Establishment to Established Nonbelief*, New York, NY: Oxford University Press.

Marsden, G. M. and Longfield, B. J. (eds) (1992), *The Secularization of the Academy*, New York, NY: Oxford University Press.

Noll, M. A. (1994), *The Scandal of the Evangelical Mind*, Grand Rapids, MI: William B. Eerdmans Publishing Company.

Patterson, J. A. (2001), *Shining Lights: A History of the Council for Christian Colleges and Universities*, Grand Rapids, MI: Baker Academic.

Sloan, D. (1994), *Faith and Knowledge: Mainline Protestantism and American Higher Education*, Louisville, KY: Westminster/John Knox Press.

Christian Higher Education – International

Arthur, J. (2006), *Faith and Secularisation in Religious Colleges and Universities*, London: Routledge.

Brighton, T. (1991), *150 Years: The Church Colleges in Higher Education*,. Chichester, England: West Sussex Institute of Higher Education.

Carpenter, J. (2008), New Evangelical Universities: Cogs in a World System or Players in a New Game? in *Interpreting Contemporary Christianity: Global Procesesses and Local Identities*, (eds.) Ogbu U. Kalu and Alaine Low, Grand Rapids, MI: Eerdmans.

Dorman, J.P. (2002), Comparing the university-level environment in the Australian Catholic university with other Australian universities, *Christian Higher Education*, 1(1), 39-54.

Glanzer, P.L. and Petrenko, K. (2007), Religion and Education in Post-Communist Russia: Making Sense of Russia's New Church-State Paradigm, *Journal of Church and State*, (Winter): 53–73.

Glanzer, P.L. and Petrenko, K. (2006), Private Christian Colleges in the Former Soviet Union (Part 1), *Church and Ministry Report*, 14: 1 (Winter): 9–11.

Glanzer, P.L. and Petrenko, K. (2006), Private Christian Colleges in the Former Soviet Union (Part 2) *East-West Church & Ministry Report*, 14: 2 (Spring 2006): 9-11.

Griffioen, S. (2002), Christian higher education in Europe: A Catholic View, *Christian Higher Education 1(2)*, 281–302.

Hulst, J.B., Ball, P. and Goheen, M.W. (eds.) (2003), *The Word of God for the Academy in Contemporary Culture(s): Proceedings of the Regional Conference for Europe of the International Association for the Promotion of Christian Higher Education*, Sioux Center, IA: DordtCollege Press.

Jenkins, P. (2002), *The Next Christendom: The Coming of Global Christianity*, New York: Oxford University Press.

Jenkins, P. (2006), *The New Faces of Christianity: Believing the Bible in the Global South*, New York: Oxford University Press.

Jenkins, P. (2007), *God's Continent: Christianity, Islam, and Europe's Religious Crisis*, New York: Oxford University Press.

Lee, J. K (2002), Christianity and Korean education in the late chosen period, *Christian Higher Education*, 1(1): 85–100.

Lutz, J.G. (1971), *China and the Christian colleges, 1850-1950*, Ithaca, NY: Cornell University Press.

Mannath, J. (1994), Higher Education In India: How Healthy Is It What Are Christian Colleges Doing? *New Frontiers in Education*, 24(4): 451.

Mejía, J. R. A. (2002), Latin American higher education at the crossroads: The Christian challenge of being transformed through the renewal of understanding, *Christian Higher Education*, 1(2): 235–51.

Ng, P.T.M. (2002), Christian higher education in contemporary China, *Christian Higher Education*, 1(1): 55–71.

Poerwowidagdo, J. (2003), Challenges to Christian higher education in Asia: Perspectives of a university president, *Christian Higher Education*, 2 (1): 35–47.

Sanneh, L. and Carpenter, J. (2005), *The Changing Face of Christianity: Africa, the West and the World*, New York: Oxford.

Schrotenboer, P.G. (ed.) (1996), *Christians and Higher Education in Eastern Europe: The Proceedings of the 1993 Debrecen Regional Conference of the International Association for the Promotion of Christian Higher Education*, Sioux Center, IA: Dordt College Press.

Son, B.H. (2002), Academic Achievement and the Christian Faith: Christian Higher Education in East Asia, *Christian Higher Education*, 1(2): 165–88.

Sutton, J. (1996), *Traditions in New Freedom: Christianity and Higher Education in Russia and Ukraine Today*, Nottingham: Bramcote Press.

Van Der Walt, B.J. (2002), The challenge of Christian higher education on the African continent in the twenty-first century, *Christian Higher Education*, 1(2): 195–228.

Lulat, Y.G.M. (2005), *A History of African Higher Education from Antiquity to the Present: A Critical Synthesis*, Westport, CT: Praeger Publishers.

Bays, D.H. and Widmer, E. (2009), *China's Christian Colleges: Cross-Cultural Connections, 1900-1950*, Palo Alto, CA: Stanford University Press.

Hartnett, R.A. (1998), *The Saga of Chinese Higher Education from the Tongzhi Restoration to Tiananmen Square: Revolution and Reform (Chinese Studies , Vol 7)*, Lampeter: Edwin Mellen Press.

Anderson, R. D. (2004), *European Universities from the Enlightenment to 1914*, Oxford: Oxford University Press.

Howard, T. A. (2006), *Protestant Theology and the Making of the Modern German University*, New York: Oxford University Press.

Rashdall, H. (1997), *The Universities of Europe in the Middle Ages*, vol 2, Powicke, F. M. and Emden, A. B. (eds.), Oxford: Oxford University Press.

Rüegg, W. (ed.) (2004), *A History of the University in Europe, vol III Universities in the Nineteenth and Early Twentieth Centuries (1800-1945)*, Cambridge: Cambridge University Press.

Rüegg, W. (ed.) (1996), *A History of the University in Europe, vol II Universities in Early Modern Europe 1500-1800*, Cambridge: Cambridge University Press.

Ridder-Symoens, H. De. (ed.) (1992), *A History of the University in Europe, vol 1 Universities in the Middle Ages*, Cambridge: Cambridge University Press.

Gerald J. Pillay

Leading a Church University

Some Reflections

The editors of this volume about leadership of church universities and colleges have requested that incumbents in this
role reflect on their own experiences. Naturally, one's reflections are often limited to ones experiences and the contexts
that shaped them. Nevertheless, these experiences undeni-
ably inform one daily — often subliminally. One cannot jump
out of ones historical skin. Yet, at the risk of sounding auto-
biographical, it may be salutary to bring experience to conscious reflection as the editors urge.

My own journey began with theological studies and the
arduous progress through the ranks from junior lecturer to
lecturer, senior lecturer, associate professor and then professor, head of department, vice-dean and dean at three universities over some 25 years; 18 of them in South Africa where
much of it was as a member of a disenfranchised minority
community under the vicious and oppressive political
system of *apartheid*. Without dwelling on these various steps

or even the political context of ones early career, at least two aspects of this South African sojourn were seminal for my present role as Vice-Chancellor of Liverpool Hope University; the first is the 'hard grind' of progressing through the ranks—the numerous hurdles to jump and committees to convince, the set-backs and the successes, the big shift from graduate student to member of the faculty alongside ones former tutors, the aspirations to scholarship and the world of peer-review (both its rigours and its perversities), the toil to establish oneself in a field, the struggle to gain the respect of older colleagues and so on—these were all formative experiences.

The world of scholarship has few analogies and an orientation into its sometimes peculiar life and habits prevents a great deal of discontentment that often well intentioned management initiatives unexpectedly stir up. For the same reasons, it is always good for designers of gardens to shore up their visionary designs with the experience of many hours digging the ground, preparing it for planting, dirtying one's hands and knowing the habits of individual plants by actually trying to grow them and observing their prospects. It's very different to learning about their habits described in a gardening encyclopaedia. Our colleagues benefit from our ability to empathise with their struggles and joys if we've walked their road as well.

The other valuable experience of these years was to learn through politically difficult times the indissoluble link there is between intellectual pursuits and the public responsibility of the scholar. This is not to argue that all theory collapses into praxis or that activism is the basis of assessing the value of intellectual pursuits; that is how revisionists or neo-Marxists often argued at that time. No, what I refer to is the lesson apartheid South Africa taught, namely, that the scholar irrespective of his or her expertise and specialism remains indissolubly interconnected with society at large and daily while negotiating a path through a veritable minefield of injustices and moral dilemmas has to live with a clear conscience; to escape into the protection of the archive or the laboratory and remain there is a cop-out. The vast majority of the intellectuals under apartheid remained relatively silent about its immorality and lived normally in an abnormal society. Theology set a wonderful example.

Being asked by the Vice Chancellor to lead the programme to help transform an apartheid-shaped university and make it fit for the emerging democracy soon to be heralded by the country's first election was a significant experience. The politics of race, fear, prejudice, anger and self-justification existed on both sides — among the beneficiaries of the apartheid system and, surprisingly, its victims. There are self-interested operators on both sides of conflict who feed on the processes of change to maximise benefits for themselves and their own side often in the terms of altruism or social justice. These proclivities cannot be learnt from text books on leadership and management but through personal encounter. It also helps to uncover ones own furtive motivations through the heat of personal ambition to the more sober judgements that come with experience and age. At least with time, one learns to judge better while being less judgemental. Taking up the appointment as foundation professor of theology at Otago University in New Zealand brought the responsibility to establish theology, hitherto located in the Catholic and Presbyterian seminaries off the campus, within a secular university—New Zealand's oldest. The prejudices of the Academy about religion and faith and the duty to form an ecumenical department have proved invaluable at Liverpool Hope University, the only ecumenical university foundation in Europe. At Hope the founding Catholic and Protestant colleges are fully integrated and, with the blessing of both denominations, remains an autonomous foundation with its own, independent Senate and Council.

New Zealand too contributed at least two key opportunities to learn. Firstly, the task to address the intellectual challenges that are put to Theology within the modern Academy now primarily shaped by a radical secularism. Secondly, to manage universities in the context of a newly liberalised market economy that followed in the wake of rolling back the welfare state.

Top-up fees were introduced in New Zealand almost 10 years before the UK even though the liberalisation of the economy in New Zealand was instigated after Mrs Thatcher's policies in the UK during the 1980s. Being a small country, New Zealand could take the experiments with the market economy speedily and radically much further than was possible in the UK. Experiencing both the benefits and drawbacks of treating higher education no longer as a public good, but a private choice based on the 'user paying', was important preparation for working in the UK with its recent trends to establish a more market-related higher education sector.

An equally formative New Zealand experience was the task to rebuild relationships between the churches, who once were providers of theology courses, and the university which was now providing these courses through its own department of theology and its own staff. Working with both Dunedin's Catholic and Anglican bishops taught a deep empathy for denominational interests while establishing an ecumenism that extended beyond mere civilities between denominational leaders or a contrived truce. How can an educational institution help fulfil the bigger mission that transcends denominational interests? What *modus vivendi* can there be on the one hand, between 'town and gown' and, on the other hand, between 'cathedral and university'. How can all three—the contenders in the public square, the Church and the University—fulfil their particular missions (or at least a part of it) together? This is a question one poses daily in the context of the modern fragmented Academy where 'society' or 'community' is experienced as an absence and Faith is relegated to the periphery or ignored.

The Ordinariness of the Task

Leading a church university in one sense carries all the demands of leading any good academic institution for advanced enquiry; yet, in fundamental ways, it is unlike leading any other kind of university. I'll explore both sides of this equation in this brief essay.

In so far as a Church university bears all the marks of the normal quest for academic excellence there is an ordinariness about our role as leaders. Ordinary but crucial nonetheless! Universities that are faith foundations do not in the main increase in recognition as places of learning by the extent or exuberance of their religiosity. They gain reputation and become sought after as universities mainly through their academic and scholarly reputation. That is why students covet places in them and why the best scholars would wish to work in them. To lead them requires a prior commitment to enhancing their scholarly status. That is a non-negotiable pre-requisite.

One, therefore, has to be sceptical of the view, popular in the 1990s, that those trained in management and leadership would bring greater efficiency to academic leadership. That was a decade obsessed with efficiency and process. It produced numerous 'airport books' on management and we all came to be enthused about 're-engineering the corporation' in word and deed. Personnel departments at universities were renamed 'human resources' departments. 'Mission' and 'vision' statements, and statements about the corporation's 'values', emerged from 'séances' facilitated by consultants—workshops where 'buy in' from staff was a precursor to published corporate plans, strategic plans and a host of other instruments by which academic institutions mimicking their corporate counterparts were 're-engineered', 'strategically downsized or devolved', 'outsourced' or 'merged'. The word 'strategic' gave a rationality to the managerialism that emerged. 'Leadership' became a new industry. A sub-class of expensive consultants and Business

Schools led this creation of the brave new world of greater efficiency and 'change management', 'quantifiable outputs' and 'key performance indicators.'

There was a view at the time that having a well-trained leader was likely to produce better results than someone schooled in a particular art or discipline; typical academics were not considered as having the appropriate 'skills set' having been trained within their fields—bright but naïve about finances and 'human resource' management. For example, someone with a MBA degree and with management experience of large and complex business enterprises could, it was assumed, run a hospital better than a clinician or a medical doctor who was never trained in leading a 'business enterprise.' The executive director of the hospital came to have as much or more power than the head of clinical practice. We now know the results of some of these experiments. Many hospitals that followed this route probably are now better managed but there is no proof that the quality of care or healing has improved, except the arguments we still hear, for example, from government departments that must take paternity for these experiments. Where there is actual improvement in the health of patients the balance of improvement must surely be largely due to the nurses and the doctors themselves (or, at least to the improvements in medical science and technology to some extent.) Only a small part of that essential quotient of progress is the result of the new experiments in management.

It is entirely possible for there to be excellently managed mediocre universities. Naturally, the 'quality movement' that has pervaded much of the Anglo-Saxon university world of the '90s (and still does) would argue that if there are adequate processes and policies in place to assure or enhance quality, then one guarantees (or least can have 'confidence') that quality can be managed and be an expected outcome. What is required, in these quality audits, is that the processes themselves are transparent, that their implementation is routinised, that validation processes are formal and regular and that the system has the necessary safeguards and measures to discern when the 'information loops' are not closed. This formal, process-driven quality approach is coherent and not without its merits. However, it does not guarantee, measure or improve quality; it probably only ensures that there would not be major failures.

Ascertaining quality requires academic judgements to be made about depth, breadth and significance of teaching, learning and scholarship and the effectiveness of the formation of the graduate. Processes, no matter how well conceived or crafted, cannot inexorably secure the scholarly conventions that have to be embedded in the culture of a university, the 'habits of the heart' of its academics and the often immeasurable transfer of ambitions and inquisitiveness that emerges from creative and personal interaction between scholars and their students; these relationships have much more to do with quality than many of the formal processes. On that measure of academic standards, therefore, leading a Church university is exactly the role of any leader of a good university; namely, to secure scholarly recognition and ensure that ones institution acquires all the hallmarks of scholarship—both in research, learning and teaching, and contribution to society.

That is easier said than done! Even in well established and well endowed research-led universities, the acquiring of excellent, research-oriented staff and the ensuring of the very best resources and equipment are an ongoing struggle. There is an ever-increasing demand for the best academics. Like the best football players, a small group can command dispropor-tionately high salaries. Attracting the best players or spotting their talent before they are ensconced elsewhere is an ongo-ing challenge.

The single most important (and expensive) task the faith foundation faces is the acquisition of the best scholars in a very competitive sector. They are not in over-abundance and in several fields are in 'short supply.' The problem is com-pounded by the elitism that exists in many countries and certainly in the UK where the better-endowed universities are also more prestigious and are able to siphon off the best from the other universities; not only because these universi-ties have more resources but also because of the natural flight to prestige. One sees this migration of scholars repeatedly before the closing dates for submissions to the Research Assessment Exercise (RAE) — the assessment which is carried out across the UK every seven years by a system of peer-review and, in future, together with research metrics (or a combination of both depending on the nature of the disci-pline being assessed.) The RAE rates research output and funds universities on the basis of their results. Normally about 12 months or so preceding the assessment deadline, there is a marked movement of staff from smaller universi-ties or less prestigious ones to the more research-intensive and more reputable. This migration exacerbates the difficulties we often experience at church foundations to retain fine scholars especially after having endured the difficulties and costs of recruiting them and, often, having paid their salaries in the years leading up to the RAE. Their work will be credited to their new institution which also receives the financial benefits that come with higher RAE results.

I shall not dwell any longer on the claim that leading a Church University Foundation is like that of leading any good university, with all the attendant difficulties. Scholarly depth is a necessary prerequisite for a good university and a leader can fail on this criterion alone.

The Academy Today

It is to the second part of our opening proposition that we turn: namely, that to lead a Christian foundation is unlike leading other universities. To begin with, the central consideration of this book about leadership in Christian higher education must be set in the context of the last 50 years or so which has seen the Academy become secularised to the point that religion has largely lost its place in public intellectual discourse within it. Matters of faith are privatised. The secularism of these years has been informed primarily by our intellectual and media elites. While most universities still have chaplains and Christian student unions, there is great unease about Religion in the Academy. It is not the intellectual unease that led, for example, to Kant's essay on the

'Conflict of the Faculties' in which he explores how Theology and Philosophy may co-exist within the University. Whatever we may make of the Kantian dualism (of *Pure Reason* and *Practical Reason*), his was a serious attempt in the context of the Enlightenment to make sense of the place of Faith within the intellectual enterprise.

Today there is no 'conflict of the faculties'—not because the conflict is resolved but because we have come to accept a form of science dogmatism. The achievement of a 'knowledge economy' and 'technology transfer' driven by an economic determinism forms the basis of a new academic propriety. Though exaggerated, that, simply put, is where we are in the Academy. A host of scholars including philosophers, sociologists and lapsed theologians feed that view. Every now and again one gets the likes of Richard Dawkins who makes it his life's work to rid the Academy, if not the world, of religion altogether. Positivism and scepticism has always existed in various mutations in society for there is no gainsaying that atheism is as old as belief and not as the secularist believes a more enlightened position after Faith is eclipsed or assailed. However, this agnosticism now forms the mainstream not the 'locus of negativity' that drives critical thought as its proponents still assume. They are in fact the conservatives now though they still think and behave as if they form the critical left.

There is an embarrassment about religious language. The discourse in the Academy, on the one hand, is pruned down to what is technical and self-evident to those in the particular discipline; often even more exclusively limited to a group of super-specialists. In the humanities and social sciences, there has emerged a class of 'logical positivists' (though they may not regard themselves as such) who shape the language of the social sciences into that which would make them more acceptable to the 'science community'; their 'science' is legitimised by graphs and statistics in the attempt to be 'empirical' and 'evidence based'. Methodological posturing takes up a disproportionate space at their conferences and in their journals to actually producing new insights into the human condition or the social predicament. A lot of the intellectual activity centres around a collection of strong interest groups each committed to their key ideological interests; they may, for example, be revisionist, deconstructionist or post-modern. Naturally, their group's interests bind them together often making them protagonists in the 'culture wars' that have raged in universities from time to time. Group interests and language create their own exclusivity and identity. These ideological interests act as 'echo chambers' to their members and further fragment the Academy.

In South Africa during the apartheid years, historians, for example, belonged to three different historical societies: a traditionalist group concerned about the history of the *volk* who conducted their discussion almost entirely in Afrikaans; the so-called 'liberal' historians who comprised the bulk of historians at English-speaking universities and the revisionists who used a neo-Marxist basis of analysis. They did not attend each others meetings and published in their own journals. They drew their lines and took their last stands against each other even while the numbers reading history at universities sharply declined and history departments dwindled.

Academic discourse is disrupted, on the one hand, by super-specialisation; on the other hand, by interest groups that can even divide departments. Relevant for our enquiry though, is the fact that the scope for religious language has been narrowed and virtually exiled to the confines of growingly smaller theology departments which are often converted into departments of religious studies. The language of Faith and its particular questions remain marginal to the pursuits of the University. The language of Faith itself has becomes defensive, apologetic and often incoherent increasing the discomfort that people of faith feel within the modern, secular Academy.

The Long View

Outside the old universities there is often an absence of the 'long view'; a historical awareness of how the Academy came to be what it is. The long view on western higher education is inextricably bound up with Christian faith which remained the case as education and learning developed through the period of the great scholastic movement, the exuberance of the Renaissance and the blossoming of art and culture in the medieval period when the first universities in the west were established; Christian Faith was at the heart of that formation. The old cathedral steeples in the great cities of Europe are a testimony to Europe's education as much as they are to Europe's civilisation and religious moorings.

In modern times, the Academy tends to represent the Enlightenment as the liberation of Reason from its imprisonment under Faith; in fact the great Enlightenment movements within the European continent were not anti-religious as they were often in the UK. For example, Rene Descartes, the father of modern mathematics and philosophy remained devoutly Catholic; Isaac Newton wrote more about the Trinity than he wrote about Physics.

The clearest statement of the Graeco-Christian 'idea' of a university is still Cardinal Newman's celebrated book which he presented in the context of 19th century Ireland when the Anglican religious test was still prevalent among the handful of universities in England. With all its contextual limitations, its ideals are still pertinent for our discussion. When Newman delivered those 9 discourses and the 10 lectures and essays that came to be the *Idea of the University* in 1852, he warned about the storm breaking from the north by which he meant the utilitarian, mercantile and industrial challenge to the Oxford curriculum. He responded with his important argument that 'knowledge is an end in itself' (Newman, 1923. Discourse V, pp. 99–123). Jaroslav Pelikan of Yale writing a book by that same name to celebrate its 150th anniversary argued that the threat to the University now comes from the 'north, south, east and west' (Pelikan, 1992, p. 11). The ideals of the technocrat, the analyst in the Treasury, the language of employer engagement with powers for users to co-design and fund degrees 'useful to them', training in skills and the like, are not new nor are they unique to us in the UK. In fact, much of it is *necessary* (and we'd be unwise not to grasp the challenges they entail) but they *are not sufficient* to the purpose of *higher* education.

That 'higher' purpose vitally includes a dedication (not in a political or ideological sense) to *liberal education* with the aim to produce what Newman described as the person who

> has learned to think and to reason and to compare and to discriminate and to analyse, who has refined taste, and has formed his judgement, and sharpened his mental vision ... will be placed in that state of intellect in which he can take up any of the sciences or callings ... for which he has a taste or special talent, with an ease, a grace, a versatility, and a success ... In this sense ... mental culture is emphatically useful (Discourse VII, pp. 165–66).

Many of the pragmatists in our times would like to think Newman's idea was esoteric and impractical. 'Education is a high word,' Newman wrote, 'it is the preparation for knowledge, and it is the imparting of knowledge in proportion to that preparation' (Discourse VI, p. 144). It was for him as much to do with 'self-education' within a nurturing community as it was about tutors teaching students in lecture rooms. (There is no doubt that church universities and colleges foundations are often known for their sense of community which outsiders recognise as distinctive.)

If the University is a place for this unfettered education with an abiding commitment to education for freedom then, I believe, the church foundation should by its nature be the first among those universities and colleges which stand up against the truncation or any narrowing of the university fashioned by whatever the prevailing ideology may be; it could be the domination of the University by the Science dogma; it could be the domination of 'outcomes based' forms of education shaped by utilitarian or functionalist purposes. It certainly must be a refutation of the notion that faith is private and that faith has no bearing on the intellectual quest. That is a difficult task in a secularised society where we've already undergone two generations of this thinking; where the secularist worldview dominates; and where the onus now shifts to people of faith to make the case for what in fact is part of that 'long view' of European civilisation. That some civic universities in this country had in their Charter excluded Theology in late 19th and early 20th century is proof that Newman's concern 50 years earlier was real.

The Church University has a *cultural and intellectual mandate* to restore that 'long view' to higher education; to hold together Philosophy, Science and Theology in the pursuit of Truth. Each helps to enlighten and offer alternatives — each is indispensible to making sense of the human situation.

Much has been written on the philosophical dimensions of religious language which need not be repeated here. What is important to be remembered for our purpose is that the affirmation of the 'language of Faith' is not merely to justify the indispensability of Religion to understand human beings; Religious language casts important insights on how we may also understand the nature and insight of Art, human motivation, Purpose and Meaning (Pillay, 2002).

The Church University by its nature protects the freedom of Science, Philosophy and Theology and nurtures them alongside each other. Their individual insights enlighten 'the

Whole', which is what the Academy (as *universitas*) is preoc-
cupied with. That is the University's *intellectual* mandate.

The Question of Distinctiveness

Another vexing question that has been repeatedly raised is
the question of 'distinctiveness.' What makes the Church
University different? To this question, the second part of my
opening statement, we now turn.

There are 14 Church colleges and universities in the UK
and its heads form a supportive group called the Council of
Church Universities and Colleges. In that Council this question has been raised repeatedly over the last 15 years. It is fair
to say that there is no common view among us. Sometimes
the link with the Church, in one or two instances, was seen as
a hindrance to shaping the institution to be more competitive
with the secular university down the road. Many of our staff
or students within the member institutions share little or no
interest in any Christian distinctiveness. Many students
probably do not even recognize that they are part of anything
distinctively Christian.

Then there are among us those who value the formal link
with the Church and its patronage—however tenuous or
'light touch' that may be; normally, ceremonial and constitu-
tional; the Church Trustees keep some oversight over the
chaplaincy or chapel life within the university and provide
valuable pastoral insight. There has been an attempt by the

Anglican foundations to describe the 'mutual expectations' the Anglican Church has of its higher education institutions and vice-versa. This document by that name appeared with not much consequence accept the reaffirmation of solidarity that the Anglican Church and its higher education institutions have with each other.

We have come to a common mind within the Council that our institutions do share a certain distinctiveness in common which we must seek out and make explicit within our institutions and publicly. To aid the latter, we have now formed ourselves into what we call the 'Cathedrals Group' to help establish a more public platform for these intentions with an inaugural launch in London in 2009 around the foundation lecture named after the late Lord Dearing. Dearing made a significant contribution to the public understanding of higher education in the UK. He himself understood deeply the need for faith foundations like ours. That said, we need still to gain clarity about the role and purpose of the Church University. What are its distinguishing features given the case above for the strong similarities between good universities?

At a meeting of heads of European Universities called during the Portuguese Presidency in Lisbon in 2007 the matter of creating a collaborative European university system within the Bologna process was much discussed and every so often there was talk of the European values that bind the European community and its universities. 'European values' were referred to quite often in the discussions and at a point on the second day of the conference one of the speakers led in a discussion on what these 'values' were. They were, according to the speaker, values such as tolerance, justice, fairness, public, administrative and private integrity. After a while these morphed into 'democratic values' and it did not take long for them to resemble what one would expect in any civilised society. Sitting there I wondered what old societies like Indian and Buddhist societies would think about values like tolerance, justice and fair play being considered 'European values' especially since they didn't have to fight major civil wars or undergo revolutions on the scale in France, to achieve them; and they also predated Europe as we know it.

In the same vein, it would be unwise to base the distinctiveness of the Church university foundation on a set of values as we too easily do. As soon as we ascertain what values are uniquely ours, we discover that they often pre-existed us in other people. Faith is not a prerequisite for morality. Hence, those without faith can commit to a humanist set of values that won't be irreconcilable to a position which people of faith could agree. We could argue that Christianity influenced humanism but that would merely confirm the view that all humanist values are Christian values; nothing then would be distinctive! The case for our distinctiveness must, therefore, be more than a statement of common values.

It is right to require any public institution, especially if it's publicly funded as all Church foundation in the UK are, to be open and welcoming of all citizens. We in this country are obliged to uphold the values of equality, diversity and such like. The Equality and Diversity Laws outlaws discrimination at that level. The question of distinctiveness is not equivalent, then, to ensuring what is deemed lawful and proper.

The Buddhists have at the heart of their thinking what they call the 'wheel of compassion' without having any doctrine of God; Buddhism being itself a non-theistic religion. They are deeply committed to the life of compassion, care for others and the sanctity of life. So even an inter-religious basis or general 'faith' basis is not enough to define what constitutes a minimum agreement for being a Christian faith foundation. The first universities in the west emerged during the 12th and 13th centuries after a 200 hundred year period informed by the Christian faith; a period of civilising the illiterate and tribal west of which the Frankish kingdom was the nucleus. In the vanguard of this process was the cathedral school initiated by Charlemagne during his cultural revolution of the Frankish Kingdom. He enrolled Alcuin of York and other Christian scholars to be the vanguard of that civilising period. The clergy themselves largely being illiterate and unable to read the Scriptures were taught Latin to transcend their different tribal affiliations and their local dialects. The oldest of the universities when they emerged cohered around the seven liberal arts and Theology led the enterprise, considered the Queen of Sciences. This influence was not merely because of the temporal power of the Church (as significant as that influence did become later) but because the Church provides the Holy Text and the sanctity of the text, available in a script and language the various dialects could read, contributed to cultural interchange and scholarship. The holy text became the generator of literacy and learning.

The modern University remains vitally engaged with the agenda that governments determine — the contribution to the public good; and that may mean finding a cure for cancer, or acquiring the next patent that will fundamentally change communications technology or biotechnology. For the church university foundation it must also mean producing the rounded graduate; the fruit of a solid education which in the end is about 'redemption' and 'redeeming the earth' of which humanity is a part and every individual a participant. That means, very simply, that we produce the kinds of graduates who leave our institutions with a deep awareness of civic and global responsibility, and with a sense of social justice. They will not always come to this understanding through overtly religious routes; but, hopefully, having been educated on our campuses they would have had an unavoidable and manifest opportunity (not an incidental occasion) to encounter more than the mundane and the routine of getting a degree qualification. This is an imperative determined by our missions. Achieving these ends in turn justifies that mission. Without it we are like any other university. Fundamentally, this mission involves the clarifying of vocation (calling) and personal formation (another deeply Christian idea.) The task to create a humane and whole (well) society is another way of speaking about 'salvation' and 'atonement' without the religious language.

We must also ask whether a Christian foundation is distinguishable from any other faith foundation because that is a question that ultimately will help us clarify this matter of Christian distinctiveness. There is much common ground that all religions share, such as, the common understanding of a moral universe, commitment to charitable works and the quest for peaceful co-existence; in these efforts we can all share in respect for each others faith. However, there is one belief central to Christian faith that constitutes a 'scandal' even to other faiths, and that is the idea of 'Incarnation'; the view that there is a breaking into human existence of divinity and that actually takes form in space and time and within history, and is personalised as Christians believe in the Christ-event. This is at the centre of Christian theology. Yet it is a stumbling block to fellow religionists that God could identify with the human condition and human predicament so fully and so humanly.

Therein is the distinctiveness about Christian institutions. Those of us who have the responsibility to lead a church foundation are called to apply our minds and our lives to finding ways to incarnate this Truth in the life of the whole institution we serve; in its ethos, its constitution, in the daily questions we raise and in the 'formation' and sometimes the 're-formation' of those who work and study with us. There is no way these tasks bear any resemblance to those of a head of any other type of educational institution, certainly not within the secularised institutions of our day. These ideas and roles are not self-evident and do not appear in any of the guidelines, which all of our universities in the UK use, whether emanating from the UUK, CUC or HEFCE[1] or such like. These are not the requirements in the auditing guides we use. The nature of incarnation requires that this Truth is made real in the life of the university and the lives of all who make up its community.

---

1   These are Universities United Kingdom (UUK), a body comprising all universities in the UK; the Council of University Chairs (CUC), and the Higher Education Funding Council of England (HEFCE).

These responsibilities we set ourselves about human society and the formation of our graduates are not incommensurate with the fundamental questions raised about how the universities can be publicly accountable; how can they give a fair return for public investment in them and what would be a meaningful 'key performance indicator' to measure it. (The church university's redemptive work is for the whole world not just for its church constituencies!)

It is interesting how the language familiar within the church has appeared in the world of the university. 'Deans', 'chancellors' and 'vice chancellors' are all borrowed from the church from where also came the graduating robes and even many of the faculty colours. More recently, though, strategic planning has mainstreamed the use of 'vision' and 'mission' statements and of self-conscious awareness of an institution's 'values.' In the handbooks for heads of university departments and guides to leadership at universities has crept the language of providing 'pastoral care' to students and colleagues. 'Pastoral care' too is fundamentally a priestly concern. It is increasingly used and while for many universities that may mean counselling and health service or support for disabled students and better 'customer service, ' for a Christian university it must also surely mean a total commitment to the rounded care and well-being of the individual student. It reflects how the church foundation actually deals with forming a community. As Newman so-well stated the university is 'alma mater knowing her children one by one; it is not a foundry or a mint or a treadmill' (Discourse VI, pp. 144–45). That is a striking way to explain why we organise and nurture the church university community, and how we aspire to maintain the well-being of every individual within it.

To summarise, there is much about the role as leader of a church university that encompasses the ordinary demands placed on leading any good university. But there is a whole area, in fact the whole rationale, of the role that is quite distinctive. To establish a strong academic foundation with all its attendant characteristics about teaching, learning and research are part of what is necessary but is not sufficient. To begin with, a church foundation true to its mission bears much of the best of the western tradition of university life. What it stands for constitutes the 'long new. It provides alongside other models of higher education a distinctive choice about the university as a community of learning that educates 'in the round' – body, mind and spirit. (This is a strap line of my own university.) Christian education nurtures a liberal education that is an education for freedom. It is unfettered freedom hence faith, philosophy and science are nurtured alongside each other. If it is goal directed then its purpose is to produce the rounded citizen with a global sense. While some universities may set for themselves solely the task of producing specialists in fields and see their role as primarily to educate for disciplinary expertise, the Christian foundation also hopes that its scholarly efforts will help to create a humane society.

Then there is the need of that distinctive awareness constantly to find ways to make real that great Truth that God who was in Christ 'reconciling the world to Himself' and who now continues that work through us and our institution

— the 'incarnational principle' that describes not just the *role* but the *task* of the leader of the church university or college.

References

Newman, J. (1923), *The Idea of the University*, London: Longmans, Green and Co.

Pelikan, J. (1992), *The Idea of the University A Re-examination*, New Haven: Yale University Press.

Pillay, G. J. (2002), Theology as a human science: reflections on Gadamer's Truth and method, *South African Journal of Philosophy*, Vol. 21 (4): 330–44.

Janet Trotter

Leadership in a Christian HE Institution

This essay is unashamedly personal and reflective. It arises from over forty years of involvement in Church Colleges and Universities as a student, a lecturer and then as Principal / Vice Chancellor.

I became Head of the College of St Paul and St Mary in Cheltenham in 1986 (now the University of Gloucestershire) and almost immediately was invited by the Chaplaincy to speak on the subject of my hopes and desires for a Church College Chaplaincy.

I selected as my text the prayer used after the communion in the Anglican *Alternative Service Book 1980*.

> Almighty God,
> We thank you for feeding us with the body and blood
>   of your Son Jesus Christ.
> Through him we offer you our souls and bodies to be
>   a living sacrifice.
> Send us out in the power of your Spirit to live and
>   work to your praise and glory.
> Amen.

The prayer speaks powerfully of nourishment, of offering, of action and of the transforming love of Christ which empowers the disciple to go out into the world to do his work.

I also referred to Paul's words in Romans 12.2: 'Be not conformed to this world but be ye transformed by the renewing of your mind' and to Martin Luther King's sermon (King, 1980) on this text in which he urges Christians to be 'transformed non conformists', committed to justice, truth and building the common good whatever the personal sacrifices.

Building on these themes I commented that here was no manifesto for the members of the Chaplaincy to minister exclusively to their own but by deeds and life style to enable others to glimpse something of the Christian vision. This general approach to the totality of work in a church institution remains valid for me today although my view of how this is manifested may have developed and deepened over time.

A recurrent and unifying theme in this essay, therefore, is transformation: The Gospel is good news which transforms individuals and situations through Christ's redemptive love and any church institution should constantly be striving through all it does to be a channel of God's transforming grace.

... By Way of Context

During the past quarter of a century or so Universities and Colleges have developed dramatically as a response to societal changes. In the 1980s all of the recognised UK Church Colleges were small with fewer than two thousand full time students. The majority of students were in residence undertaking teacher training programmes and entered higher education immediately following secondary education. These Colleges were cohesive, intimate institutions: staff student ratios were high and students felt members of a community where they were known and which had a particular ethos and set of underpinning values. The chaplaincy was at the centre of this community, often physically, and the majority of students and many staff were drawn into its fellowship. While society generally was becoming more diverse and secular these institutions appeared homogeneous, anchored primarily in a particular tradition which drew students to them. In these circumstances the Principal was an observable embodiment of the institutional values, supporting the chaplaincy and the life and work of staff and students.

The changes of the past twenty or so years have made the task of the Head of the Church College / University more challenging. All of the UK Church institutions have expanded dramatically, some in excess of tenfold. Many now operate across several campuses, some thirty, fifty or even one hundred miles apart. Many of the students are part time rather than full time learners, some undertaking distance learning programmes with little need to visit any physical part of the institution itself. Some are taking programmes overseas. Additionally, many students and staff have not selected to join the institution for its particular Church association but for a variety of other reasons, for example, location.

The small, intimate community has, in these circumstances been blown apart and institutional leaders have had to reflect on how the founding traditions of their organisations can be manifest in an environment of supercomplexity and change. What was nurtured in the small, intimate, relatively informal communities of the past cannot be sustained in the same way in the modern institution. More deliberate and formal structures and approaches are necessary if students are to glimpse a vision of God that is both attractive and transforming.

I will explore some of the formal structures and approaches developed at the University of Gloucestershire (and its predecessor colleges) under the following headings:

- the institution: its vision, mission and values
- the chaplaincy
- the curriculum

Finally, I will consider the question of leadership and set this within the framework of organisational transformation.

The Institution:
Its Vision, Mission and Values

In 1990 the College of St Paul and St Mary in Cheltenham
merged with the higher education programmes of the
Gloucestershire College of Arts and Technology (GlosCAT).
Both institutions had academic strengths but the vehicle for
the merger was the governance arrangements of the Church
College. The relevant Trust Deed, dating from 1847, was to be
continued: it was avowedly evangelical following the
churchmanship of the prime mover, the Reverend Francis
Close. It stated:

> It is solemnly intended and purposed that the religious
> education to be conveyed shall always be Scriptural,
> Evangelical and Protestant and in strict accordance
> with the Articles and Liturgy of the Church of Eng-
> land, as now by Law established, in their literal and
> grammatical sense, and that these principles should
> for ever be preserved as a most sacred trust at any sac-
> rifice of pecuniary loss or temporal interest.[1]

The students and staff of GlosCAT, which was avowedly secular, were suspicious of the Church connection and of this
formulary and the fine art students took to the streets fearful
of censorship and a loss of academic freedom. Meanwhile the

---

1   Foundation Trust Document quoted in More (1992).

staff of the Church College were anxious that their community and ethos would be undermined.

In these circumstances it was particularly important to establish a vision and mission around which the new College could cohere and discussions at the time were dominated by a wish to draw the best from the traditions of the past and to use these as a springboard to transform our collective future. Energy was created by openness to doing something different based on a re-interpretation of the original Trust Deed accepting that it is the responsibility of each generation to study founding texts and make them live for their day. It was recognised that the death of two institutions was involved in the merger but also the possibility of new birth and new life.

The governing body, in consultation with staff and students set up a small working group with the task of developing the vision, mission and values of the new College. The group studied the concepts and realities of higher education via such thinkers as John Henry Newman, A. N. Whitehead and those associated with the origins of the Gloucestershire Colleges. It pondered A. N. Whitehead's view that

> the University imparts information, but it imparts it imaginatively: the atmosphere of excitement, arising from imaginative consideration, transforms knowledge. A fact is no longer a bare fact: it is investigated with all its possibilities (Whitehead, 1929)

and John Masefield's work of 1946 in which he says of higher education,

> It is a place where those who hate ignorance may strive to know, where those who perceive truth may

strive to make others see: where seekers and learners alike, banded together in the search for knowledge, will honour thought in all its finer ways, will welcome thinkers in distress or in exile, will uphold ever the dignity of thought and learning and will exact standards in all these things (Babington Smith, 2008).

After much debate and reflection the following values statement gained consensus within the new college and, with minor variations, has continued to be at the forefront of the vision and mission of the institution.

The College / University will be:

- excellent but not inaccessible

- Christian but not exclusive

- nurturing but not constricting

- proud of its locale but not parochial

The words in each phrase recognised not only the complexity of the educational environment but also the dialectic or tension in being true to the past while also being open to the future.

The College clearly wished to be excellent in all it did but it did not conceive this in elitist terms. Accessibility also needed to be pursued and it set about changing the unusually middle class complexion of its student population and succeeded in terms of ethnicity, social background, gender and age, although there is still much more to do. It is, perhaps, worth noting that the original 1847 Church Training College in Cheltenham was the first such institution to train men and women side by side in the UK so accessibility and equality were principles valued by the founders although today we might not recognise as such some of the practices pursued.

In relation to 'Christian but not exclusive' the College embraced its Christian tradition: it knew its roots and what nourished its life. However, in the light of the Gospel it wished to provide opportunities for faith to be explored, to be rigorous intellectually and pedagogically, to be neighbourly to other traditions and to provide gracious hospitality to all. In the spirit of the latter the College developed a range of relationships with Muslim organisations, including the Association of Muslim Schools, with a view to supporting its educational institutions.

'Nurturing but not constricting' set out the aspiration to support and develop the potential of all students: it was recognised that this necessarily involved risk, openness and exploration and that the College should not inhibit the learning journey of students.

The phrase 'proud of its locale but not parochial' was designed to recognise the importance of thinking globally and acting locally. From the early 1990s the College sought to work within Gloucestershire to be part of its social and economic transformation while recognising that we are all global citizens and need to take our responsibilities to sustainability seriously. From this point the curriculum was increasingly designed to raise the global dimensions of subjects studied, new buildings were developed on sustainable principles, green transport plans were introduced and attention was paid to reducing the carbon footprint.

This values statement led to heated debate over time about where the emphasis between the various elements should be placed but one of its strengths was its ability to provide continuity and to highlight to staff and students those key principles valued by the College in the past and in the present, and which provided direction for the future.

The Chaplaincy

There is no question that the Chapel is at the heart of the Church institution and, with the Principal / Vice Chancellor and senior team, is a subtle part of the leadership framework. It is here that the life and work of the College / University is offered to God: it is here that prayer takes place for the needs of the world: it is here that the (often) small community of Christians comes together to be renewed and refreshed. Daily worship is important but at Gloucestershire, because of the nature of the academic programmes and its multi campus nature, it has become increasingly difficult to create the sense of a gathered, worshipping community although cell groups for prayer have flourished.

In such a setting, however, the chaplaincy has a particular ministry to the whole organisation whether individuals are, for example, Christians or enquirers, atheists or Muslims, secularists or Hindus. For this reason the chaplains must be in the market place where people are: where there are moments of crisis and tension and where students and staff both celebrate and face the ultimate issues of life and death. They must be seeking opportunities to be prayerfully engaged in activities and processes, open to the possibility of transformation.

Such engagement can be evidenced in, for example, painstaking work with students, families and staff to create an appropriate memorial service following the tragic death of a student or member of staff. It is often the case that those involved do not have the language or emotional resilience to handle such issues and the chaplains can help and support in ways which are long remembered.

On other occasions the Chaplaincy has organised discussions and debates drawing in staff and students from a variety of disciplines represented within the academic community. Particularly lively events have been held on the interface between crime and punishment and the concepts of social justice, consumerism and euthanasia. Throughout, the aim was to inform, to raise ethical issues and to engage participants in matters of fundamental importance to the future of society.

Larger scale projects have also demonstrated particularly how the chaplaincy has a key role in working with the institution to progress its vision and mission.

Opening a new campus in a new location is always a challenge. How will it develop? How can the desired ethos be established? How can it be supported to contribute fully to the development of the whole organisation?

When the College opened a new campus dedicated to sports programmes it decided, as part of establishing the chaplaincy on site, to appoint two young sports people who were also Christians to work with the students and link the work of the campus to its local community. These were essentially training posts, supported by the Rank Foundation, and were designed for young adults wanting to explore their faith in a youth / sports context. The two young men appointed had a profound influence on the successful development of the campus. They were extra-ordinary role models running events in conjunction with the Student Union, working in local primary and secondary schools as part of the widening participation agenda, participating in youth groups across the county, holding prayer meetings and professing their faith in all they did. Students had daily reminders of Christianity at work in the lives of contemporaries via prayer, reading the Gospel and social outreach.

It is perhaps, significant that one is now attached to a church in full time Christian ministry and the other, having completed further study, is a lecturer at the University. From these chaplaincy and foundation initiatives the Campus has developed an MSc in Christian Ministry and Sport and has appointed its first professor in this area.

Secondly, the chaplains made the chapel a place of gracious hospitality. In one year the Chaplaincy sponsored a fine art exhibition on the theme of Genesis and engaged students in the Biblical stories of creation in addition to those of other religious traditions and scientific theories. The resulting work, which transformed the somewhat austere early twentieth century Chapel was innovative and inspirational, with many students claiming to have paid close attention to the Biblical text for the first time. In a similar vein, around the time of the Gulf War, the chaplaincy invited creative writing and fine art students to use the Book of Lamentations as a stimulus for their work. Concurrently the chaplains, a Writer in Residence and a small group of students worked with prisoners at Leyhill Open Prison in South Gloucestershire on the same theme. The evening of sharing and occasional tearfulness was one of mutuality and extending horizons, a genuine standing in the shoes of others whether in the Gulf, in prison, in the time of Jeremiah or as a student in a late twentieth century College.

Thirdly, the chaplaincy has been involved in community outreach and active promotion of social justice. At times students under the aegis of the chaplaincy have been involved in running homework clubs for local children who would otherwise not have been able to study with appropriate support. Acting as mentors they provided significant encouragement to the many socially deprived children around the campuses.

Through prayer, study, worship and activities such as these the chaplaincy demonstrates its engagement with the University's vision and mission and opens itself and the community to the transforming work of the Holy Spirit in its life and work.

The Curriculum

The core business of a publicly funded church HEI is the planned curriculum and at Gloucestershire pedagogy was mission related and issued in a number of special awards to staff and departments (e.g. National Teaching Fellowships and Higher Education Academy awards).

As noted above recent decades have brought a new set of challenges to higher education. It has been said that this century may well be one of relearning on a grand scale: the old certainties have been swept away and with them the approved ways of seeing and understanding shaped by language, culture and personal experience. It is true that there is a bewildering array of conflicting views, ideas, values and life styles evident around us and in this context HEIs must equip their students to play their part in shaping the world in new and different ways.

This responsibility is set out starkly in the United Nation's Millennium Declaration signed in September 2000.

> We have a collective responsibility to uphold the principles of human dignity, equality and equity at the global level ... the central challenge we face today is to ensure that globalisation becomes a positive force for the world's people.[2]

When the College in Gloucestershire (now University) was formed it wanted to make the planned learning that took place transformational. Innovatively for the early 1990s a modular curriculum was introduced to help students themselves design their curriculum, to produce combinations of subjects and themes which suited them and to be open to risk and experimentation in a supportive structure. It

---

2 *United Nations Millennium Declaration* (2000). Resolution adopted by the General Assembly 55/2.

also included at an early stage a skills element which incorporated the exploration of values and issues related to sustainability, in addition to information and language skills.

Transformational Learning can be defined as learning that takes knowledge and skills into a different domain, with a step jump in the cognitive and affective process. The theory of transformational learning has been described as 'the process of making meaning of one's experience'[3] and is often traced back to Paulo Freire's consciousness raising among individuals and groups in the middle of the last century while also teaching them to read. During this process the learners developed the ability

> to analyse, pose questions and take action on the social, political, cultural and economic contexts that influenced and shaped their lives. Through dialogue and problem-posing, learners developed a deeper understanding of how social structures can shape and influence how they think about themselves and the world (Dirkx, 2000).

Researchers into Transformational Learning have subsequently suggested that it can be divided into three phases including critical reflection, reflective discourse and action. Mezirow has suggested that engaging in such a process can result in

> frames of reference that are more permeable to amendments ... and overall more emotionally capable of change as opposed to acting upon the purposes,

3   Pedagogical Research and Scholarships Institute: Research Briefing, 10th June 2009, University of Gloucestershire.

values, feelings and meanings we have uncritically assimilated from others (Mezirow *et al.*, 2000).

Sometimes setting the learning in a different context is supportive of developing such new frames of reference. At Gloucestershire, for example, some students visited Uganda annually as part of their academic programme. They trained voluntarily all year prior to departure to support the development of information technology skills in a teacher training College in Kaliro, a rural area. As part of their academic programme while in Uganda, students used their disciplinary skills to, for example:

- write a business plan for the Ugandan College for a proposed new information technology qualification for graduating teachers
- research the impact of waste management practices and lack of sanitation on groundwater quality in villages in Uganda
- investigate perceptions of water quality by Ugandan hand pump users

Many students claimed on their return to have found the experience life-changing in terms of being enabled to see the world through new eyes: many also committed themselves to development projects and to sustainable lifestyles.

Other students from disciplines such as geography, literature, theology, history and landscape architecture undertook a module on Holocaust Landscapes which was designed annually to explore how events are memorialised in particular landscapes (e.g. the massacre at Dunblane, the site of Fred West's atrocities and genocide in the 1939–1945 war). On one occasion I registered for the module. The classes in Cheltenham raised the key issues via films and the reading of novels. This was by way of preparation for visits to Auschwitz, Treblinka and Warsaw where we witnessed the museum to holocaust victims at Auschwitz and the magnificent, stark sculpture at the forest clearing in Treblinka representing a host of Jewish, men, women and children, trudging to their slaughter. At our nightly suppers we were debriefed and also had opportunities to meet individuals involved in the events. I remember particularly a man whose parents had, like Schindler, sheltered young Jews, helping them to escape eventually to the UK and the USA. His father had died as a result and as he spoke he sobbed saying he was speaking in detail of these things which had been locked, unspoken in his memory, since that time. Many of the participating students found this encounter hard to bear: witnessing the painful memories of another brought the consequences of war vividly to life for them.

In the final debriefing and in the personal diaries they wrote during the module it was clear that the students knew more about the second world war: stereotypes had been challenged and they were more conscious of the devastating effects of demonising a race of people of a particular colour, creed or gender. They also made links to their world: to genocide in Bosnia, Kosova and Rwanda and to issues of justice and equity in Britain today.

A change of context can produce transformational learning as the vivid examples above demonstrate but so can learning which places emphasis on engagement with material in new and different ways, seeking out deep meanings and consequences for lives as lived today. In this context case studies, role-modelling, real-time projects and problem based material can be particularly illuminating and transforming.

The Leadership Task

In his book *Leadership: A Critical Text* (2008), Simon Western criticises organisational cultures such as Enron and its accountants Arthur Anderson which have displayed a corporate culture that overrides individual agency, transparency and autonomy.

He puts forward the view that leaders of the twenty first century must

> create and support ethical frameworks for leadership in practice. This means helping leaders identify organisational structures, processes and forms of communication to promote individual agency and autonomy alongside collective solidarity. This aim should comfortably align itself with progressive and now mainstream contemporary organisational aims, which include corporate responsibility, sustainability, clarity of vision and strong values, non exploitation of employees and outsourced workers, and ethics as integral to commercial and output success.

For Western modern leadership is marked by strong networks, connectivity and organic sustainable growth which acknowledges the human spirit, the power of the imagination and the importance of human relationships. Such leadership favours devolved power, the dispersal of leadership and 'having the confidence of not knowing, of being able to follow emergent patterns, rather than fixed plans' (op. cit.).

Western's analysis is helpful in the context of exploring leadership issues in a Church institution. Here the governing body has a responsibility to set the strategy, tone and style of the organisation but the Principal / Vice Chancellor and his or her senior team have a major role in ensuring they are operationalised.

Heroic, authoritarian and bureaucratic styles of leadership are inappropriate in an organisation which claims a Christian foundation. The Vice Chancellor and the senior team always need to act in the light of the Christian values espoused, devolving power, developing healthy relations, seeking organic sustainable growth and fostering corporate responsibility: in effect, supporting the transformation of the organisation and those associated with it by providing opportunities for God's grace to flow through its life and work.

This requires the careful recruitment, induction and development of staff in which the leadership needs to be fully involved. It also involves the valuing of all staff whether support or academic.

This leading of an organisation for transformation requires both courage and creativity. Accepting old orthodoxies unquestioningly must be viewed as inappropriate and there must always be a vision of new possibilities both locally and globally.

At Gloucestershire, recognising this, we were one of the first adopters in higher education of an annual report which focussed on corporate responsibility and set out our pedagogical and volunteering work with students, our links designed to regenerate communities, our staff research into, for example, the environment and business ethics and our commitment to reducing our carbon footprint.

Academic freedom must also be positively encouraged, the status quo must be rigorously questioned and collegiality must be promoted. On reflection I am particularly proud of the work Gloucesteshire undertook with the staff unions. Initially relations were poor with suspicion and ill will on all sides. By conversation and genuine commitment to the best interests of staff we managed to create a healthy mutual respect which worked to the good of all. On several occasions the Chair of the major academic union and I shared a national platform on the benefits of such partnership.

I am aware that not all staff or stakeholders would commend all of my decisions: not all would see my leadership style as transforming. For me, however, it was important throughout my tenure to keep testing out conclusions and recommendations in the light of the evidence and to bring them prayerfully to God seeking his direction and strength.

'...Send us out in the power of your Spirit'

It was one of those quiet July evenings at the end of the academic year when the President of the Student Union visited me. Her degree programme had ended and she was about to embark on her Sabbatical Presidency. As the shadows lengthened she asked why I did what I did and what motivated me. She commented that my Christian faith was apparent but wanted to know what my own journey had been. We talked long into the evening about issues of life and death; of hope and despair; of incarnation and redemption. During the following year I witnessed her faith grow and when she left she decided to take a course designed to strengthen her Christian discipleship and then work in the mission field in Brazil. She returned to the UK some twelve months later to join the West Midlands police force, her faith still strong and her commitment to building the Kingdom of God unwavering.

On another occasion, the day of my University retirement party, I found a somewhat crude African drum placed on the desk in my office. The accompanying note informed me that it was the gift of a student who had been to Uganda on several occasions. The experience had been transformational for her, particularly witnessing the ravages of HIV / AIDs on the young children of rural communities. On her return to the UK she had been committed to developing a project for the boys of Uganda. This involved putting safe sex slogans on footballs to make the boys and young men have access to such messages via a medium they accepted. The drum had been bought from a small group of HIV/AIDs orphans seeking to make a living in a rural community. The project continues and the gift was, perhaps, the most fitting and memorable of all those I received on my retirement.

The drum which I still keep in my study symbolises for me that Church Higher Education Institutions can and should offer nourishment (physical, intellectual, spiritual and moral) to those who come to them and in turn send them out into the world to be transformed non-conformists.

Some will, of course, do this in the name of Christ while others may not name or know the source of their inspiration. What the leadership of the Church Institution must, however, ensure is that in the totality of the organisation's life and work opportunities are created for the spirit to 'blow where it wills'.

References

Babington Smith, C. (2008), *John Masefield: A Life*, Stroud: The History Press.

Dirkx, J. M. (2000), Transformative Learning and the Journey of Individuation. ERIC Digest No 223.

King, Martin Luther, Jr (1981), *The Strength to Love*, Minneapolis, MN: Augsburg Fortress Publishers.

Mezirow, J. and Associates (2000), *Learning as Transformation: Critical Reflections on a Theory in Progress*, San Fransisco, CA: Jossey Bass.

More, C. (1992), *The Training of Teachers 1847–1947*, London: Hambledon Press.

Western, S. (2008), *Leadership: A Critical Test*, London: Sage Publications.

Whitehead, A. N. (1929), *The Aims of Education and other Essays*, New York: Macmillan.

Michael Wright

Church Universities

The Leadership Challenge

Introduction

The challenge arises from the need to communicate
Christian values in a collegiate life which is open to all
and which does not resort to petty coercions for the
purpose. This requires a sensitive pragmatism in all
things which strives to maintain the visibility of
Christian values in ways which make their acceptance a matter of free choice. much has to depend
upon accumulated tradition, sensitivity and common
sense.

These are the words of Revd Dr John Elford who, at the time
they were written (1989), was the Head of St Katharine's
College and Pro-Rector of the Liverpool Institute (now Liverpool Hope University). They were included in a book

celebrating the first 150 years of the Church of England's Colleges of Higher Education.[1] The 'challenge' to which he refers is the task of leading such an institution.

In 1997 I took up post as Principal of what was then Canterbury Christ Church College, the first of only two Church of England Colleges established in the twentieth century (1962), the other being St Martin's Lancaster founded in the following year. The significance of the 1989 book for me was that it — and specifically Elford's contribution — was really the only preparation which I was able to undertake for that specific part of my role which was concerned with sustaining the College's position as a Church Foundation. Whilst I had enjoyed excellent experience, advice and preparation for the job in terms of general higher education leadership, my reading of Elford's contribution to the book was the only significant material I could find on what being the leader of such a college might involve as opposed to descriptions of the history and purposes of such colleges. Although much had and has subsequently been written about the history, structure, purposes and governance of Church Colleges and Universities in England and elsewhere,[2] I could find little which addressed the specific challenge of leading a college or university with a Church Foundation, and especially one founded by the Church of England. John Elford helped to fill that gap for me and what I felt I lacked in the quantity of my preparation was offset by the quality of his contribution, a contribution which was enhanced by my subsequent conversations with him. In the years following my appointment to

1   Brighton (1989). The Elford quotation is on p. 15.
2   For a comprehensive bibliography, see Arthur (2006), pp. 160–69.

Canterbury I have also greatly benefited from the discussions I had with my colleagues in the Council of Church Colleges and Universities especially during our annual residential conferences.

Ten years after my appointment to Canterbury Christ Church, by now a University, a discussion with the Pro-Chancellor (Chairman of the Governing Body) led to the suggestion that I should have a short sabbatical during which I would reflect on my experience as Principal and Vice Chancellor. More specifically, I would consider the nature of leadership in a university with a Church Foundation and prepare a paper which could benefit others facing the challenge of such a leadership role. The study was not intended to be either comprehensive or scientific but instead an opportunity to reflect on the experience of those, including myself, who had held the post of 'chief executive' of such an institution.

During the six weeks of my sabbatical (early 2008) I read or re-read books and articles on Church colleges and universities, had conversations with fellow Vice Chancellors or Principals of several Church universities and colleges in both England and South India and reflected on the issues. In the discussions I explored the ways in which those in leadership roles ensure that the university or college addresses not only its higher education purposes but also its mission as an institution with a Church Foundation and how those different aspects can be held together and integrated. Further, I was interested to learn of ways in which the Vice Chancellor or Principal demonstrates, both internally and externally, that the university or college is a distinctive higher education institution and to gather views on the qualities and skills thought to be necessary to enable the role to be fulfilled effectively. This chapter is essentially a reflection of what I have learned during the past twelve years including reflections arising from my sabbatical.

Some History

It is not the purpose of this chapter to consider the history of the Church's involvement in higher education. However, as in most matters, an understanding of what has gone before helps to put the present position in context and, in particular, provides the background to the challenge of leadership. Since Canterbury Christ Church was founded by the Church of England, it is therefore worth summarising the history of the Church of England's involvement in higher education.

In England the Church led the way in the provision of education — and other social services — long before government came to regard itself as the predominant provider. Schools and hospitals were established by parishes and individuals as a response to the Gospel message of love and concern for people irrespective of their faith or beliefs. The school which stands next to the Canterbury campus of Canterbury Christ Church University — King's School Canterbury — is generally considered to be one of the oldest (if not the oldest) in England with its origins in the mission of Augustine to Canterbury around AD 600. Many schools were established in subsequent centuries well before the introduction of elementary education for all in the 19th century. For older scholars, dating back to pre-Reformation times, many of the colleges of the universities of Oxford and Cambridge reflect their Christian origins in their names as do many of the hospitals in which the nation's doctors are trained. In the 19th century King's College London (1829) and the University of Durham (1832) were founded as a result of action by the Church of England. The extent to which these institutions remain Christian in their characteristics and practices and, perhaps more importantly, in their governance and leadership arrangements vary but most continue to have traditions and chaplaincy arrangements which reflect their history as religious institutions. Conversely, those universities founded on explicitly secular principles have often introduced practices which recognise that those who attend or work in them should have the opportunity to consider the spiritual dimension of being human.

Arising from the significant growth in school education, principally as a result of action by the Church, by the beginning of the 19th century the Church of England recognised the need to establish teacher training colleges for those who would work in the schools and did so through the work of the National Society and local dioceses. The first recognisable Church College was founded in Chester in 1839. Funds for building the colleges were largely provided by the Church whilst, as an indication of the partnership between Church and State, running costs were increasingly met from the public purse. Staff and students were expected to be active members of the Church of England and each college's chapel was a central feature of daily life. In the sixty years which followed, the number of such colleges grew to over thirty. Other Christian denominations also established similar institutions to meet their own requirements. In the early 20th century the number of places in the teacher training colleges was expanded and some of the colleges relocated to new places and premises. However, no new colleges were established after 1899 until the 1960s when, partly in response to the need for more teachers, Canterbury Christ Church and St. Martin's Lancaster were founded. By this time general expectations of all the church colleges in relation to church involvement had begun to diminish although governance and leadership arrangements continued to reflect the Church of England's 'ownership' of all the colleges with the Principal usually being ordained and the Chairman of the Governing Body often being the Diocesan Bishop. Although they had grown, all of the colleges remained small in comparison to the growing number of universities and higher education colleges and they continued to be exclusively concerned with teacher training.

The 1970s witnessed dramatic changes in both higher education generally and specifically in teacher training. The decade saw the emergence of local authority polytechnics and a sharp decline in the number of teacher training places. Many teacher training colleges, both Church and secular, closed whilst others were subsumed within larger and more diverse universities and polytechnics. In some cases the closing Church Colleges were able to secure special arrangements in the acquiring institution e.g. chaplaincy provision or professorial posts. With the benefit of hindsight it would appear that these various special arrangements generally failed to maintain the distinctiveness of the provision of the former Church College. It is suggested that this may reflect the fact that, without the committed (Christian) leadership which only a chief executive and an autonomous and appropriately constituted governing body can provide, the Christian purposes of an institution will be at risk.

In response to the changing context of higher education during the past twenty-five years, the autonomous Church of England Colleges which remain (nine in number with two others being part of ecumenical institutions) have generally diversified and grown to the point where, in curriculum terms, they are in some cases apparently indistinguishable from so-called secular universities although all continue to have teacher education as an important part of their provision and many now include or have strengthened their work in health and social care. Most have also extended their work in academic theology and are involved in clergy and lay training. The majority of the former Church Colleges are now universities in their own right having successfully demonstrated that they meet the relevant criteria. There are however a number of ways in which they are or consider themselves to be distinctive. Examples are set out in the report 'Mutual Expectations' (2005).

A Distinctive Contribution

Whilst not strictly relevant to this chapter, a few comments about the contribution which Church universities and colleges make to higher education and to the work of the Church may be relevant. Although I have done no serious research on the topic, it is arguably the case that there probably never was a clear articulation of the reasons for the Church's involvement in higher education because it was apparently not necessary. When the Oxbridge Colleges and, in later times, the Church Colleges were founded, there was an implicit expectation that those who attended would be either Christian or sympathetic to Christianity and that the authority of the leaders to speak about its Christian purposes would not be questioned. The existence of institutions with a Christian ethos was part of the educational landscape and no justification for them was necessary. Indeed it has been suggested that questions about the distinctiveness of the colleges founded by the Church or of their curriculum were simply unnecessary since the very existence of the college itself represented the curriculum.

In more recent times and with the changing influence of the Church in society, questions have inevitably and properly been asked about ways in which the Church universities and colleges are distinctive and in a position to contribute not only to higher education but also to the work of the Church of which they are a part. In 2001 Lord Dearing chaired a group which reviewed Church of England schools and colleges. In the report of the group's findings ('The Way Ahead', 2001) Dearing recommended that the colleges (many are now universities) should strengthen their character as distinctive and inclusive Christian institutions and, in particular, offer clear encouragement to those seeking to work in schools. An appendix to the report sets out a template for the distinctive features which should be found in a Church higher education institution.

Leadership Issues in Theory

The nature and challenge of leadership is one of the 'hot' topics of our time. In relation to the private, public and voluntary sectors, a great deal has been written as to what, in theory and practice, constitutes effective leadership. In different sectors, organisations have been founded with the specific purpose of improving leadership practice. Such organisations include those which focus specifically on leadership in the Church, perhaps the most recent being the 'Foundation for Church Leadership'. The Foundation publishes papers and organises conferences including one held in February 2007 at which I was invited to deliver a lecture on leadership in higher education.[3] In it I reviewed the various main theories of leadership, Christian perspectives on the

---

3   Conference papers published in *Exploring Team Leadership* (2008).

subject and sought to apply those theories to my experience and vice versa. In particular I compared and contrasted my role with that of a parish priest. Whilst there are clearly some differences, especially in terms of scale and purpose, the fundamental challenge of leading a university is similar to that of a parish priest or, arguably, to that of anybody charged with leading a 'people organisation'. A copy of my presentation to the conference is attached as an appendix to this chapter.

In 'Mutual Expectations' (op cit, paragraphs 72 76) it is asserted that if a church university or college is to be able to be distinctive in Christian terms, it must be governed and led by people who have heard and understood the Christian call to reach out and engage in dialogue. At the same time it is recognised that the leaders and governors must also be able to understand and exercise the skills associated with the wide range of legal, financial and related responsibilities involved in running increasingly large and complex organisations. In particular it is suggested that the leadership of the Vice Chancellor/Principal is 'vital' since he or she must be able 'to articulate and implement a clear vision of a church higher education institution'. It is for this reason that many of the church universities and colleges retain, as the law allows, a 'genuine occupational qualification' based upon the individual's faith position, albeit differently expressed in relation to the individual institutions. A more open question is the extent to which institutions impose similar requirements to other postholders and whether the law will uphold such requirements for postholders other than the chief executive.[4]

Based upon his extensive international research, Professor James Arthur (2006, pp. 137–38, 149–50) clearly sets out his views of what constitutes effective leadership of such an organisation and of those actions which threaten its religious identity. He identifies the need to ensure that a clear majority of the trustees or governors are committed members of the religious community in question and suggests that the church in question should hold residual powers over the institution's assets. Of the leader, he suggests that he or she will need 'to understand the nature and purpose of their faith's philosophy of education, be able to articulate this vision, inspire others with it and have the ability and courage to establish and sustain that faith identity in their college or university. In a sense, they need to be leaders not only of their college or university but leaders in some sense of the faith community as well. They will consequently insist that religion has a central place in the life of their institutions and will help to build a community in which the faith development of all is integrated into the ethos and curriculum. The religious dimensions of their leadership will never be seen as additional but central to their task of leading'. This clearly represents a daunting challenge but is one with which I readily agree.

4   See 'A guide to governance in church higher education institutions' (2007).

Leadership In Practice

In the course of my time at Canterbury Christ Church I have discussed the challenge of leading a Church-related university with a number of colleagues with a similar role. In preparing this chapter, I have added my own views to those of the other Vice Chancellors and Principals. These views are obviously set in the context of English Church-related universities.

In many Church universities and colleges, although the individuals concerned had worked in higher education for a number of years prior to taking up their present post, few had previously worked in a Church higher education institution or are ordained ministers. This contrasts sharply with the previous generation of Church College Principals who, in almost all cases, had spent a number of years in this part of the higher education sector and were often ordained. For each of those to whom I have spoken and for me, the opportunity to lead a university or college with a Church foundation was a very important reason for seeking or accepting the appointment. Prior to being interviewed for their current post most had limited knowledge of the work of the Church Colleges believing, as many people continue to believe, that they were concerned only or mainly with teacher education. In their opinion, it continues to be the case that the Church

Universities continue to find it difficult to make their work known more widely, not least within the Church.

A common experience of the Anglican Principals to whom I have spoken and to me, is that we have all become more personally involved in the Church than we had expected. Whilst we had all been previously involved in our respective parishes in different ways, the opportunities to become Lay Canons, Lay Members of Cathedral Chapters, members of Diocesan Synods etc have been greatly welcomed both for themselves and because such activities represent an opportunity to strengthen links and to reinforce the Church University in local Church life. However we were all generally surprised to find that there was a lower level of Christian commitment amongst staff than we had expected and that the Church was less aware of its local higher education university or college than we had hoped. That said, we have all found those local Church people who are aware of our work to be supportive. We have all sought to sustain and strengthen the work of the chaplaincy recognising that this is a particular way in which the distinctiveness of the University can be demonstrated.

In exercising our leadership roles, most have found it especially helpful to be able to discuss the particular challenge of leading a Church University with senior colleagues, Governors and fellow Vice Chancellors and Principals. However we recognise that, given the legal constraints surrounding religious beliefs and the perceived limitations on extending the genuine occupational qualifications concept, it may become increasingly difficult to ensure that there is a sufficiently large group of committed senior staff with whom the task of providing Christian leadership can be discussed and shared. In response to a question about the desirable personal qualities of such a leader, there was a shared view that it requires the ability and willingness to articulate a clear vision for the institution, to build relationships within both higher education and the relevant faith community, to be confident about our personal faith position and willing to share it, to demonstrate a personal and institutional commitment to the values of the university and to recognise the importance of being inclusive because we are Christian rather than, as it is sometimes presented, despite being Christian. All of us would have valued an opportunity to participate in a structured programme designed to address the needs of newlyappointed Vice Chancellors or Principals of institutions with a Churchrelated mission. Such a programme could be organised by the Church and/or the institutions themselves with contributions from those with appropriate expertise and experience.

In the course of my discussions with fellow Vice Chancellors and Principals, it became apparent that we all share reservations about some current higher education policies and believe that our institutions have a part to play in counterbalancing some of the more excessive aspects of these policies. In particular, the perceived shift towards a view that higher education's principal purpose is to serve economic imperatives sits uneasily with the Church's reason for being involved in education. The very reason for founding our colleges was clearly 'vocational', the training of teachers, but we have concerns that a number of apparently unrelated policies may combine to squeeze out of the curriculum time and space for wider concerns which are at the very heart of being human. Each of us recognises that we have an obligation to address such concerns although none of us has an easy answer to the question.

Reflections and Conclusions

In reflecting on the issues arising from my time at Canterbury Christ Church, the most obvious one is that the Church should draw satisfaction from what has been achieved as a result of its decision to involve itself in the provision of higher education. Oxbridge has been at the heart of the English university system for 800 years and, during the past two centuries, the Church Colleges have made a substantial contribution to the education system of the country initially in relation to teacher education and more recently on a broader basis. The Colleges have faced significant challenges at various times in their history most especially in the 1970s and 1980s when their very survival was a real concern. The fact that those which remain have survived and developed is both a cause for celebration and a reason to acknowledge the leadership of those who had the task of leading them during those difficult times. This is certainly true of those who led Canterbury Christ Church at that time, creating a sound platform upon which further developments could be built.

It is apparent that there continues to be some uncertainty in the Church of England as to what it expects of those uni-

versities which are related to the Church. Mutual Expectations was an attempt to explore this but appears to be
regarded as having not quite achieved its stated purpose of
setting out the expectations which the Church and the institutions have of each other. That said, given the independence
of the institutions, their different histories and circumstances, the diocesan structure of the Church and changing
attitudes in society and in law towards religion and religious
belief over the past fifty years, it is unlikely that a single view
could easily emerge. Perhaps the most desirable outcome is
to recognise that the institutions each make an important
contribution to the work of the Church and, if they are to
continue to do so, it is essential to ensure that, in their governance and leadership arrangements, the Church must retain
a strong influence. In this context, the recent experience of
forming the University of Cumbria is interesting and it will
be worth considering, in say five years time, how the
structures and practices which have been put in place
have enabled that University to sustain its Christian
distinctiveness.

What is clear from both the literature and from conversations with my fellow Vice Chancellors is that the role of the
Vice Chancellor in sustaining the ethos of the institution is
crucial. It is a task which can be shared but it cannot be dele-
gated. This represents a significant personal and professional
challenge. In talking to one of my fellow Vice Chancellors we
reached the view that it is important to set that challenge in
the context of the time in which it is exercised. Earlier generations of leaders were responsible for establishing colleges
which were small and had a limited range of activities but

they established an ethos and a way of doings things which often remain at the heart of the institutions into which they have evolved. In more recent times the challenge was essentially one of survival and required the ability to be what might be described as a 'principled entrepreneur'. This required the ability to lead the process of diversification and growth whilst having regard to the need to ensure that the Christian values of the institution were sustained in what was in any case a changing environment in terms of both higher education and the church in society. In the past ten or fifteen years the challenge has been to enable the former colleges to take their place in the university sector whilst at the same time responding to changing expectations on the part of a range of 'stakeholders', among them the Church. The conclusion which can be drawn from this is perhaps quite simply that the obligation of the Vice Chancellor or Principal is to ensure that the continuing 'threads' of the Church college or university are sufficiently strong that they can be pulled through by his or her successor

As a final thought, it seems to me that what ultimately matters in deciding whether a Church University is appropriately distinctive is not what is done or even how it is done. In the end, as Elford wrote, what matters is that the work which is done in the University and all the other activities which take place in its name reflect the Gospel message of love. Members of the University and those who engage with us should continue to be encouraged to understand that this is our purpose.

References

Arthur, J. (2006), *Faith and Secularisation in Religious Colleges and Universities*, Abingdon: Routledge.

Brighton, T. (ed) (1989), *150 Years: The Church Colleges in Higher Education*, Chichester: WSIHE.

Reports etc.

'A guide to governance in church higher education institutions' (2007), Council of Church Colleges and Universities.

Exploring Team Leadership, Foundation for Church Leadership, ISBN No. 0955057310 (2008)

'Mutual Expectations', The Archbishops' Council of the Church of England, GS1601 (2005).

'The Way Ahead: Church of England schools in the new millennium', Church House Publishing, GS1406 (2001).

APPENDIX

Foundation for Church Leadership, 1 February 2007

Team Leadership in Higher Education

The word 'leadership' is an often used, perhaps overused, term which is capable of drawing forth a huge range and variety of opinions as to its meaning. The preparation of a short talk on the topic certainly presents no problem with regard to reference material. By spending less than ten seconds at my computer, the 'Google' search engine offered me 169 million references for leadership. A visit to an ordinary public library reveals the large number of books on the subject and a trip to the business and management shelves of an academic library does so to an even greater extent. In one recent year alone, 187 books and articles with that word in the title were published. Many other more general books include chapters on the topic. These books and articles contain models, theories, diagrams, statistics and advice in an attempt to provide a convincing answer to two fundamental questions. Firstly, what constitutes effective leadership and, secondly, which individuals can be regarded as effective leaders?

Whilst I can only claim to have read a tiny proportion of the published literature on the subject, what I can say with some certainty is that neither question can be answered definitively. Books on leadership are not like those on the legal or financial aspects of business where relatively concrete information and advice is possible. They are not even like ones on organisational behaviour or project management which reflect measurable outcomes in differing situations and circumstances. Books on leadership should probably occupy that section of the library reserved for questions such as 'what is love?' or 'how to make yourself happy'. I say this not to be dismissive of either of those important issues or of attempts to analyse the elements of effective leadership but simply to indicate that opinions on this topic are ultimately subjective.

However, since I have been asked to do so, I must try, but given that there is no shortage of literature on the subject, I have decided to reflect on my actual and practical experience of leadership in higher education rather than to offer yet more theories. That said, it would be somewhat odd for someone who has spent his life working in universities to suggest that theoretical perspectives are unimportant. It is therefore worth noting that, since leadership is such a well-researched subject, there are even books which offer a synopsis of other books on the topic. One such is a small book by John van Maurik (Writers on Leadership, Penguin 2001) in which he summarises the writings of over thirty acknowledged experts on leadership including John Adair, Meredith Belbin, John Harvey-Jones and Jim Collins. The analysis by van Maurik reflects the main theories of the past sixty years or so including those which stress the importance of assessing the traits or qualities of successful leaders, those which rely upon the idea that adopting the right behaviour is the key, those which recognise the importance of changing leadership styles to reflect changed circumstances and the most recent, the so-called transformational theories, which combine elements of the others but which also emphasize the importance of team leadership.

So, why is leadership such a difficult concept to define or explain? The answer surely lies in understanding the importance of the context in which leadership is being exercised. Without that understanding, an assessment of the effectiveness of leadership styles and qualities is well-nigh impossible. Hence to attempt to speak about leadership in higher education — together with any possible lessons for leadership in the Church – in an abstract fashion or a vacuum is almost a contradiction in terms. The other main challenge is to decide whether to speak in the first or third person – as an authority on the subject or as an observer. To do the former is to risk being accused of immodesty whilst to do the latter may seem too self-effacing. On balance, I have decided to risk talking in the first person with the declared proviso that you obviously cannot know the context in which I have worked but I must invite you to assume that I did.

When I was invited to nominate a title for this paper I chose 'team leadership in higher education' principally because this is the most significant leadership role I have had. That said, being President of a tennis club or, as I currently am, Captain of a golf club can present formidable leadership challenges. Such challenges may actually be particularly relevant to Church leadership given that in sports clubs one is largely working with volunteers over whom one has virtually no authority of any tangible kind although I will return to the issue of volunteers later.

As you know, I am neither a management theorist nor a theologian. What I am is a Grammar School boy, brought up within sight of Durham Cathedral who read law at University, entered academic life and, thirty five years later, finds himself as Vice Chancellor of a University with a Church of England Foundation. During those thirty five years, twelve were spent teaching law, fourteen in a senior management role below chief executive level and the past nine as chief executive reporting to a governing body. Along the way I guess I have learned something about leadership both by observing others and from my own experience. Whilst mindful of my earlier comment about immodesty, I—and I think others—feel that my leadership has generally been successful, to this point at least although each day brings new challenges. However, that statement rests upon two enormously significant contextual conditions, the 'culture' of higher education generally and the particular circumstances of the organisations in which I have exercised leadership.

On the first issue, the culture of higher education, there are understandably many features of life in universities which make it very different from other sectors although perhaps not entirely dissimilar to the Church. Those who participate in it—the students—do so entirely voluntarily and for all sorts of different reasons. Those who work in universities do all kinds of different work in support capacities such as administration, finance, personnel, catering, estate management or manual work and the particular context of their work (i.e. higher education) may be of lesser importance to them. On the contrary, many academic staff are committed first and foremost to their subject and to their students with the particular requirements of their employing university, being, in some cases, of secondary importance. It is this characteristic which gives rise to the opinion that trying to organise academics is akin to herding either cats or elephants. Undoubtedly an important feature of academic life—as with the Church—is the accepted practice of staff feeling entitled to comment on any issue without fear of reprisal. This concept of 'academic freedom', which can pose particular leadership challenges, has become increasingly difficult to balance against the growing legal and quasi-legal restrictions on freedom of speech and action in relation to race, gender, sexual orientation, religious belief etc.

The other important contextual condition, the particular circumstances of the organisation at the time in question, is equally significant since leadership must reflect specific needs. What I have learned about myself is that it is both easier and more satisfying to exercise leadership in an organisation which is developing and growing and where a 'can do' mentality prevails and, conversely, a more challenging test of leadership arises when unpleasant change is needed especially when such change may not apparently seem necessary to those being led.

As a Christian I have naturally asked myself about the theology of leadership, whether secular theories are relevant and what part prayer plays. The secular theories include numerous references to leadership from the front, from behind and even from the side. Here of course we find resonance with the concept of 'servant leadership' the idea that in order to be a leader, he or she must be a servant. In Mark Chapter 10 verse 42, Jesus says 'You know that among the Gentiles those whom they recognise as their rulers lord it over them but it is not so among you . Whoever wishes to become great among you must be your servant and whoever wishes to be first among you must be slave of all. For the Son of Man came not to be served but to serve .' What does this mean for a Christian seeking to exercise leadership in a large organisation? In my view, it means two things in particular. Firstly, the idea of servant leadership does not demand a particular style of leadership but reminds me that I must have an abiding appreciation of the purpose of the University and the needs of those whom we seek to serve, the students, together with the needs of those whose work helps students to achieve their goals. It is therefore imperative that in all I do and say I should look at issues from the perspective of students and staff. Secondly, servant leadership means that I should never forget that all my colleagues have needs which are no different from mine, hence, for example, there is no justification for me to expect to travel first class if standard class is the norm.

In addition, however, given that Canterbury Christ Church University is both a University and a Church of England Foundation, that fact adds an additional dimension to my leadership role. Here I come to what I believe to be the similarity between my role and that of a Church leader, perhaps especially a parish priest rather than a Bishop. A number of years ago I was asked to speak on the topic of Leadership to the Parochial Church Council of the Church within which the University's main campus is located. At the beginning of my talk I identified the apparent differences between the parish and the University, most obviously in terms of our basic purpose and in terms of scale (the University has an annual budget of £80 million, employs 1500 staff and owns an extensive property portfolio). I then sought to consider the similarities, the chief of which include

(a) being part of the Church of England albeit in different ways;

(b) the importance of volunteers in our work, the members of the Governing Body being unpaid and the contribution of staff being willing to work beyond their day to day duties;

(c) long term plans being susceptible to short term pressures;

(d) communication being a constant challenge;

(e) the overloading of people not least as a result of the modern tendency of involving (or perhaps appearing to involve) people in every decision;

(f) busy people being far too busy;

(g) what that parish priest called 'superficial work' i.e. the perceived need to be seen to do things rather than necessarily to do them well (in the case of the University, a sense of obligation to respond to every Government initiative);

(h) our respective sizes, a 'parish' in both cases of ten to fifteen thousand people with a 'roll' of two to three hundred people;

(i) for me and the priest, a feeling (right or wrong) that we must personally undertake many tasks including ones which could equally effectively be done by others.

I then went on to offer some thoughts on how I exercise team leadership, the key points being:

(a) recognising that very few, if any, people have gifts in equal measure, it is important to identify the strengths of each individual in a team, allocating tasks which play

to their strengths and, as far as possible, relieving them
of others;

(b)   the importance of what I call 'walking about', it being
essential that those being led meet their leaders where
they are — formal meetings and paperwork have their
place but have their limitations;

(c)   the importance of building a leadership team in which
all members share corporate responsibility but have
clearly understood individual roles and responsibilities.
Regular meetings of the senior team (eight people in the
case of the University) are essential (weekly in our case)
as a vehicle for sharing the outcome and direction of the
team's work BUT it is even more essential that their
individual decisions are trusted and not constantly
reviewed. I know from personal experience that there is
nothing more demoralising than to have every decision
taken twice especially if the decisions are different;

(d)   the importance of clear communication throughout an
organisation with an organisational structure which
facilitates effective communication. The challenge of
communication or the perceived lack of it is a constant
cry in most organisations, the irony being that the problem seems to increase in direct proportion to our techno-
logical capability in this area. It is generally accepted
that the optimum 'span of control' is between ten and
twenty people and the same goes for effective communication systems. Department sizes in Universities tend to
reflect this and, in a Church context, I believe that the

Church of Scotland's model — the Kirk Session and the elders — has much to commend it.

All that I have said comes together in the analogy which I most often use to describe my role. I liken my role to that of the conductor of an orchestra, harmonising the contribution and gifts of the individual sections and players, ensuring that there is more or less sound at different times from the strings, woodwind etc and, at the end, acknowledging either the applause or the lack of it but recognising that it is really for the players.

In closing, however, there is perhaps more than meets the eye in the opinion of the 19th century French revolutionary politician, Alexandre Auguste LedruRollin: *Je suis leur chef, il fallait bien les suivre* — 'I am their leader, I really ought to follow them'.

Joel Cunningham

A Few Stories and a Small Quilt

When Vice Chancellor Wright invited me to contribute to these reflections on leadership in Christian higher education, I was both honored and daunted. I have enjoyed serving with him on the Board of Trustees of the Colleges and Universities of the Anglican Communion, which he chairs, and was eager to support his efforts on this project, but I was cautious about my ability to provide new or useful perspectives. In the end, my enthusiasm for joining in the project outweighed my reservations.

As I write, I have begun my twenty-sixth and final year of serving as the vice chancellor or president of a university tied to a church body. From 1984 to 2000, I was president of Susquehanna University, a Pennsylvania institution affiliated with the Evangelical Lutheran Church in America, and in 2000, I returned to my home state of Tennessee to become vice chancellor of a unique institution of the Episcopal Church, the University of the South in Sewanee, Tennessee. In midsummer of 2010, I will retire as vice chancellor but continue as a professor of mathematics.

My family roots go back seven generations in rural southern Middle Tennessee, not far from Sewanee, and I have
decided to take some liberty in these reflections by combining two of the chief components of friendship and community in these parts: story-telling and quilt-making. First I will
offer something of a rag-bag of stories, and then I will quilt
together some observations and counsel that arise, at least in
part, from those stories.

Story 1: Sewanee

From its earliest beginnings, the University of the South, or
Sewanee as it is more often called by those who love it, has
had the Episcopal Church at the center of its governance. Its
charter, granted by the state of Tennessee in 1858, specifies
that 'The University ... shall in all its parts be under the sole
and perpetual direction of the Protestant Episcopal Church,
represented through a Board of Trustees.' That now-150-
member Board comes principally from the twenty-eight
dioceses of the Episcopal Church across the South of the
United States—from Florida to Texas and from North
Carolina to Missouri; and it includes the bishops of those
owning dioceses as well as a presbyter and two lay trustees
from each of them.

Located on 13,000 acres of mountain and cove land at the
western edge of the Appalachians, Sewanee's academic-
gothic sandstone buildings—with the soaring All Saints'

Chapel at its center — remind visitors of the architecture of Oxford and Cambridge. The University has a substantial endowment supporting its highly regarded undergraduate liberal arts college and distinguished graduate School of Theology; it enrolls between 1500 and 1600 students, including approximately 75 seminarians. Sewanee is marked by intense collaboration between faculty and students, and by close, lifelong friendships among students and between students and faculty. These, together with Sewanee's striking architecture and abundance of forests, streams, caves, and trails, set the University of the South apart as one of the gems of American higher education. One indication of its distinction is that Sewanee's total of twenty-five Rhodes Scholars is higher than those of all but three other liberal arts colleges and most large research universities in the United States. The University draws outstanding students from all over this country and around the world, and it stretches and strengthens them to be prepared for lives of high achievement, thoughtful reflection, and dedicated service.

Sewanee's Episcopal character is much in evidence in many ways, including through the liturgical form of all University convocations, the wide array of weekly worship services, the theological scholarship and the formation of priests in the School of Theology, and the prominent roles of the Chancellor, who is a bishop of one of the owning dioceses and chair of the Board of Trustees, and the Chaplain, who is one of the University's most senior officers. However, Sewanee has also long welcomed students, faculty, and staff from other backgrounds, including Christians from other traditions, Jews, Muslims, Hindus, Buddhists, agnostics, and atheists. Although the primary focus of the School of Theology is on preparing priests for the Episcopal Church, it also serves some students seeking to become Methodist ministers, Lutheran pastors, and clergy in other denominations.

Story 2: My Church Roots and Professor George Connor

My father and mother met as students at David Lipscomb College in Nashville in the mid 1920s. They had both grown up as what were called Campbellites, members of the Church of Christ, a Christian congregational grouping that had arisen in and just west of the Appalachians, in the early nineteenth century, seeking to recover the Christian faith as it was practiced in the first century. The Church of Christ held, with great force, for the authority of the Bible, adult baptism by immersion, godly living, and simple services with *a cappella* hymns and weekly communion. One of my early church memories is of my father admonishing me to sit still during a Sunday-morning sermon at the New York Avenue Church of Christ in Oak Ridge, Tennessee, when I was four or five. He said, 'Joel, if you can't quit squirming, I'll have to take you out and spank you.' I tried for a few minutes, but gave up and whispered to him, 'Please take me out and spank me,' which he did.

I never knew exactly why—despair at the prospect of my bad behavior in church might well have been a factor—but my parents decided, within a year of that spanking, to leave the Church of Christ and join a newly-formed congregation, First Christian Church of Oak Ridge. The Christian Church, or Disciples of Christ as it is known more formally, shares many of the same Campbellite roots of the Church of Christ but was seen by my parents as being less severe in its demands, more open to ecumenical ties with other church bodies, and less certain about Biblical interpretation.

That migration was the last for my parents; they became pillars in the new congregation, but their having moved from more certainty to less somehow started me on a trail of seeking that did not stop there. Having been baptized in the Christian Church as an elementary school student, I became a Baptist in junior high and high school, and then tried a few other denominations, depending at least in part on who was willing to date me at the time.

In college, I made the rounds of a good many more churches — Baptist, Christian, Presbyterian, Lutheran, Episcopal — and for a time sang in the choir of Chattanooga's First Methodist Church, but it was not until a faculty member took it upon himself to invite me to church that a path began to become clear. George Connor was then an assistant professor of English at the University of Chattanooga; he later received the University's highest honor as a Guerry Professor, but when he first called me into his office in the spring of my freshman year in 1962, to enroll me in an honor society for students who had done well on their first college grades, he still shared an office with two other faculty members. He welcomed me warmly and congratulated me gingerly, with a warning that early success in college could be fleeting. He asked if I had decided what course of study to follow. When I told him that I was thinking of majoring in psychology and becoming a lawyer, his face took on a somewhat pained expression, and he said something like, 'Mr. Cunningham, you seem to have some promise. I hope you will consider doing some serious work here.' His expression lightened only a little when I responded that I thought I might also major in mathematics.

I am not sure whether it was in that conversation or a later one for some now forgotten purpose, when, at that same desk, Mr. Connor asked me, 'Do you go to church?' Feeling a little crowded by the question, I stammered that yes, I did go to church but, having visited several since arriving on campus, I had not yet settled on one. The facial expression that this response elicited was a much happier one, and in a flash he had invited me to come with him to his Episcopal parish, St. Peter's. Shortly thereafter, Trudy Bender—the woman who took me as her husband a few years later and has graciously kept me ever since—and I began attending confirmation classes there. When the rector accepted a new call soon after, Professor Connor took over teaching those classes in addition to his weekly teaching of what was surely one of the most demanding, thoughtful, and literary Sunday School classes ever in the world. We were generously adopted by the parish and were soon confirmed there. George Connor was a devoted friend, helpful advisor, and inspiring example from those early years until he died in 2002. The instances of my debt to him are far too numerous to recount. He hosted us in his home. He took me to Sewanee on several occasions; once, in August of 1964, to hear the controversial lay theologian William Stringfellow, and once in 1978, when we sat literally at the feet of Archbishop of Canterbury Michael Ramsey in Sewanee's Guerry Auditorium. George wrote us long, thoughtful letters in the years we spent in Oregon, Kentucky, and Pennsylvania. We read his weekly columns in the St. Peter's parish newsletter religiously.

In 1973, George was the matchmaker in bringing us back to Chattanooga, making the rather outrageous suggestion that the Chancellor might want to invite a struggling young mathematician at the University of Kentucky to head a new continuing education initiative for what had by then changed from private to public status as the University of Tennessee at Chattanooga. Mr. Connor, more than any other, welcomed us, with our two young daughters, back into the life of St. Peter's Church, including pulling me into serving twice on the vestry, once as parish treasurer, and once as Christian education chair. George nominated me to be academic vice president at Susquehanna University in 1979 and president there in 1984. He drew us into a happy friendship with his good friend, the famed writer Frederick Buechner, and he gave generous encouragement when Sewanee's vice chancellor search committee took an interest in me in 1999. On the feast day of the Epiphany in January of 2000, he came to Sewanee, bringing two priests who had also been dear friends and mentors for Trudy and me, to be available to reassure any doubters among the Trustees of the University of the South that, even though I had fallen in with Lutherans in Pennsylvania, I would be a worthy choice to be Sewanee's vice chancellor. And just a few days before the stroke that ended his life, in August of 2002, George drove to Sewanee for a wide-ranging lunch conversation, about higher education and the future of the Church, with me and Fr. Samuel Lloyd, former Chaplain of the University of the South, then Rector of Trinity Church, Copley Square, in Boston, and now Dean of the National Cathedral.

It is safe to say that I would not think or write as I do, have the values I hold, or love the Church as I do, were it not for George Connor. Although I have been blessed to have had many splendid teachers, he was my teacher and mentor more fully and steadily than any other. As he did for many others, he led me to many great writers, among them St. Augustine, Shakespeare, T. S. Eliot, William Temple, Alan Paton, C. S. Lewis, Flannery O'Connor, Eudora Welty, Madeleine L'Engle, Anne Tyler, and Frederick Buechner. And it was a heavy moment indeed when it fell to me to follow his careful instructions for his funeral Eucharist and read the passage he had selected from the Book of Revelation in his beloved King James Bible.

Story 3: Strains in Church Ties at Susquehanna

I became Susquehanna University's academic dean and vice president in 1979. The University's president was a distinguished scholar of American education, Jonathan Messerli, who then was beginning his third year there, having earlier served as dean of education at Hofstra and Fordham Universities. He was a brilliant, hardworking, highly dedicated man. He drove hard for what he saw as in the University's best interest, and he sometimes struck sparks with those who saw it differently.

Susquehanna was one of the colleges and universities of the Lutheran Church in America (LCA), which was one of the three national Lutheran church bodies (the others being the American Lutheran Church (ALC) and the Association of Evangelical Lutheran Churches (AELC)) that from the late 1970s were working to merge into a single new body, the Evangelical Lutheran Church in America (ELCA), which came into existence in 1988. The LCA was headquartered in New York City and included synods and parishes across the country stemming largely from early German immigrants and later Swedish ones. Susquehanna, along with three other Pennsylvania colleges — Gettysburg, Muhlenberg, and Thiel — had arisen from German Lutheran roots in the early and mid-nineteenth century. Like these sister institutions, Susquehanna was tied to the church through financial contributions from a variety of church organizations, student recruiting opportunities in parishes and synods, strong chaplaincies, strong choral music programs, and service by trustees designated from the church on the institutions' governing boards. However, over many years, the membership of those boards had become quite diverse, paralleling changes in patterns in the student bodies and faculties of these schools, with increasing numbers of non-Lutherans. As the national Lutheran Church bodies worked through the many aspects of the merger, there were corresponding issues on college campuses. Many of the colleges of the ALC, such as St. Olaf College, had governance systems that were ultimately subject to endorsement by the ALC's Churchwide

Assembly, whereas at Susquehanna and many other LCA colleges the governing boards were free-standing and church-designated board members were in a minority. For a variety of reasons, not least being the growing generosity of donors with no ties to the church, tension developed occasionally over how Susquehanna's character as a church-related institution should be expressed. From time to time, one group or another of faculty, students, alumni, donors, church leaders, or board members raised concerns about public statements that attempted to summarize the ties between the church and the University, with some urging stronger expressions of those ties and others pressing for greater distance between the two.

In 1979 and 1980, a commission drawn from the LCA's Central Susquehanna Synod and its two church-related colleges, Gettysburg College and Susquehanna University, developed a new 'Statement of Partnership' for the colleges and the synod. In preparing this statement, the drafters worked to find an acceptable middle ground between those who longed for the earlier more sectarian character of the colleges and those who preferred that these institutions focus more fully on goals shared with secular institutions such as academic distinction and cultural diversity. The resulting statement, which was adopted by each of Gettysburg, Susquehanna, and the synod in 1980, included a section (II-D) that not long thereafter came under fire from several Susquehanna board members. That section read:

> The colleges will acquaint each present and prospective member of the faculty and staff with the nature of the church-college relationship and make every effort

to employ persons who are supportive of this relationship and sensitive to the importance of the religious dimension in life. The synod will honor the
colleges' need for and right to employ the best
qualified persons with a diversity of religious
perspectives, while at the same time assisting the
colleges to identify candidates who have a Christian
commitment.

The concerns, which came from both Christian and non-
Christian Susquehanna board members, focused on the
dissenters' sense that the language of section II-D might lead
to undue influence from the synod on faculty hiring. In 1982,
Susquehanna's board withdrew its acceptance of that one
section in the partnership statement and asked the other
parties to join in finding a substitute. Donald Housley in his
2007 *Susquehanna University 1858-2000: A Goodly Heritage*
described what followed as '... a long, drawn-out, and sometimes dramatic controversy about the college's prerogatives
and the Church's expectation' (p. 504). President Messerli,
who already in 1979 had been embroiled in heated exchanges
with church leaders when the synod reduced its financial
support for its colleges, gathered an impressive advisory
committee chaired by Krister Stendahl, then the dean of the
Harvard Divinity School and later Bishop of Stockholm, to
lay a theological foundation for an alternative to section II-D.
Stendahl's resulting document drew on Luther's doctrine of
the Two Kingdoms and asserted the value to the church of
being tied to colleges that are academically vital and have a
diverse faculty and student body. Based on the Stendahl
report, President Messerli worked with other administrators,

including me, to prepare an alternative to II-D, but, in June 1983, the synod's annual assembly, after debate marked by strongly critical comments, rejected its executive committee's recommendation that the alternative be adopted. This left the partnership statement and, to some degree, the whole relationship between Susquehanna and the church in a fractious limbo that frustrated most everyone involved. The goal of renegotiating section II-D was never achieved. President Messerli left Susquehanna to become president of Muhlenberg College in 1984, and I became Susquehanna's acting president and, in 1985, its president. The attention of the Central Susquehanna Synod of the LCA was diverted to the hard work of merging the LCA into the new ELCA. Tempers cooled. Housley recalls Susquehanna board chair Erle Shobert's address to the 1984 synod assembly asking, on behalf of the Susquehanna board, that the ties between the University and the synod be preserved and that further consideration of section II-D be delayed at least until a new Susquehanna president could be appointed, and Housley adds that 'Acting President Cunningham signaled a new day in the college's church relations when he informed the board's committee on Religious Interests that "our church relations would be marked by being of service to the Church rather than arguing with the Church"' (p. 507).

James Burtchaell in his mammoth 1998 book, *The Dying of the Light*, gives a passionate, scholarly account of what he sees as a steady erosion over many years of the ties between American church bodies and many of their colleges. In his chapter on Lutheran colleges, Burtchaell recounts the II-D story from a somewhat different angle and cites Gettysburg and Susquehanna as examples of institutions whose character as church-related colleges has dwindled (489–500). My own sense is different. In my years at Susquehanna, the ties there seemed to me to grow rather than dwindle as Burtchaell saw it. A distinguished retired Lutheran pastor, Raymond Shaheen, consented to serve as special assistant to the president through all my years as Susquehanna's president and continued with my outstanding successor, L. Jay Lemons. Susquehanna Chaplains Christopher Thomforde and Mark Radecke gave excellent leadership in worship, pastoral counseling, and community service. Church gatherings were welcomed warmly. Library resources and continuing education were provided as resources for Lutheran pastors. Spectacular choral church music was a hallmark of the University. I served actively for many years on the board of a large regional Lutheran social-service agency and in several national Lutheran groups, including a term as chair of the ELCA college presidents' organization. It was a special honor when in 2000 at my last occasion of serving as host for a large Lutheran assembly on the Susquehanna campus, shortly before I left for Sewanee, Bishop Donald Main of the ELCA's Upper Susquehanna Synod introduced me as the first-ever honorary member of the synod. Even if he had been there, James Burtchaell would probably not have been impressed, but I have to admit to having paused to recall how different that occasion felt than had my first defensive appearance representing Susquehanna at the LCA's Central Pennsylvania Synod's annual assembly in 1984. When I got back to my seat, an old friend leaned over and whispered in my ear, 'Not bad, for a thinly-veneered Episcopalian.'

Story 4: Sewanee's Purpose Statement

From early in its history, Sewanee welcomed students, faculty, and staff from diverse backgrounds, Christian and non-Christian, although until the late 1960s all students were required to attend chapel. When alumni from before that time gather, the stories often turn to the methods the University employed to compel that attendance and, in some cases, the lack of complete success therein.

As is customary in American higher education, Sewanee's system of governance delegates to the faculty the chief responsibility for determining the University's curriculum, and it delegates responsibility for organizational and budgetary matters to the administration, under the oversight of an executive body, the Board of Regents, that acts on behalf of the Trustees.

Sewanee's faculty is both highly distinguished and quite diverse. Decisions about criteria for faculty appointments and the arrangements for faculty searches are handled primarily by continuing faculty members in an academic discipline, in consultation with the Dean of the College, and the focus is on recruiting the best possible teacher and scholar. This works well for the most part and has given Sewanee a faculty in which the Trustees and Regents take pride.

However, from time to time, not surprisingly, some Trustees or Regents, whose aspirations for the University relate to the needs and interests of the church, see issues from a different angle than some faculty members, whose aspirations relate more to academic considerations. An example of such a difference in viewpoint developed in the work that began in 2004 to renew the University's statement of purpose.

Sewanee's Strategic Planning Committee, whose members include faculty, students, and administrators, had the responsibility for overseeing preparations for the University's every-ten-years report to and evaluation by its primary accrediting body, the Commission on Colleges of the Southern Association of Colleges and Schools (SACS), which was to be completed in 2005–06. One of the expected steps in that work was a review of the University's statement of purpose, which had last been revised in 1993, prior to the last SACS review. The statement is included prominently in the University's official catalogs and read, perhaps less often than one might imagine, by persons who are first becoming familiar with Sewanee, including prospective students and their parents.

The Strategic Planning Committee concluded that the statement as adopted in 1993 should be revised to be, as one member put it, more engaging, less old-fashioned, and more gracious. The Committee asked the University's Chancellor, Bishop of Alabama Henry Parsley, to chair a drafting group that included Dean of the College Rita Kipp, Dean of the School of Theology William Stafford, and distinguished poet and Carlton Professor of English Wyatt Prunty, with support from Provost Linda Lankewicz and me. That group worked through the 2004–05 academic year to develop a proposed revision, which the Strategic Planning Committee endorsed and forwarded to the Joint Faculties for consideration in April 2005.

The Joint Faculties endorsed the proposed new statement, judging it to be an improvement from the 1993 one and recognizing that delay at that point would make it impossible to have a revision in place before the 2005–06 SACS review. However, the faculty asked that work be continued, with additional faculty participation, to deal with the concern that the statement did not adequately reflect Sewanee's commitments to welcoming people of differing backgrounds, including those of many different religions and none. The Regents endorsed and the Trustees adopted the new statement in May 2005, understanding that there was likely to be a proposal for further changes.

Over the next two years, official and ad hoc groups, along with the original drafting group, wrote and traded drafts. I had a sense of déjà vu from the early 1980s at Susquehanna when the debates about section II-D were at their heaviest.

At Sewanee, all involved recognized that there were some fundamental differences in focus and concerns among the many individuals and groups involved in this work and that the ultimate decision would be that of the Board of Trustees, but the original drafting group listened carefully to the many somewhat different voices over more than two years, drafting and redrafting.

In the end, a statement was put forward by the group chaired by Chancellor Parsley that modified the statement adopted in 2005 to affirm more clearly the University's commitment to welcoming people of diverse backgrounds.

Some would have preferred other changes, but the new draft was endorsed by the Strategic Planning Committee, the Joint Faculties, and the Regents. It was adopted by the Trustees in October 2007 at their meeting at which the University's 150th anniversary was celebrated.

I considered including here some samples of the many contending drafts and arguments that were considered along the way in this process, but space is limited and, more importantly, I suspect recounting the conflicting views would be likely to do more harm than good. Hence, following the lead of my fellow mathematicians, who most often show their readers only a patched and polished end result rather than airing the rough work that lies behind a proof, here is Sewanee's statement of purpose as it stands since 2007 and will until some other brave souls come along to try to improve on it:

> The University of the South is an institution of the Episcopal Church dedicated to the pursuit of knowledge, understanding, and wisdom in close community and in full freedom of inquiry, and enlightened by Christian faith in the Anglican tradition, welcoming individuals from all backgrounds, to the end that students be prepared to search for truth, seek justice, preserve liberty under law, and serve God and humanity.
>
> The College of Arts and Sciences is committed to the development of the whole person through a liberal arts education of the highest quality. Outstanding students work closely with distinguished and diverse faculty in a demanding course of humane and

scientific study that prepares them for lives of achievement and service. Providing rich opportunities for leadership and intellectual and spiritual growth, while grounding its community on a pledge of honor, Sewanee enables students to live with grace, integrity, and a reverent concern for the world.

The School of Theology educates women and men to serve the broad whole of the Episcopal Church in ordained and lay vocations. The School develops leaders who are learned, skilled, informed by the Word of God, and committed to the mission of Christ's church, in the Anglican tradition of forming disciples through a common life of prayer, learning, and service. Sewanee's seminary education and world-wide programs equip people for ministry through the gift of theological reflection in community.

Story 5: The Colleges and Universities of the Anglican Communion

The Colleges and Universities of the Anglican Communion (CUAC) traces its history to the formation of the Fund for Episcopal Colleges in 1962 and its incorporation as the Association of Episcopal Colleges (AEC) in 1966, with a board of trustees that included the presidents of the American colleges and universities with ongoing ties to the Episcopal Church. AEC's founding executive was Arthur Ben Chitty, who was a mainstay of the University of the South before and after his AEC service in New York City, having served the University as a fundraiser, co-editor of *The Sewanee News*, author of several books on Sewanee, and, until his death in 2003, University's historiographer. Through the efforts of Mr. Chitty and others, substantial gifts were received by the Association, including endowment funds that by 2000 had market values totaling more than $2 million. In spite of those resources, the presidents of AEC's member institutions had become somewhat less engaged in its work by the early 1990s, and the Trustees reached out to colleges and universities with ties to church bodies in the Anglican Communion around the world, with the result that a new association, the Colleges and Universities of the Anglican Communion (CUAC), was formed, with shared offices with the AEC. The leaders for this initiative included AEC President Linda Chisholm, CUAC General Secretary John Powers, and the chair of CUAC's board of trustees, David Peacock, Principal of Whitelands College in England.

I attended my first meetings of AEC and CUAC trustees in New York City in the spring of 2000 soon after I was elected as Sewanee's vice chancellor but before I took office. Since then I have been a trustee of both CUAC and AEC and have participated in the transitions that brought Donald Thompson, former Principal of Thornloe College in Canada, to be Linda Chisholm's and John Powers' successor as CUAC and AEC's General Secretary and of the succession of CUAC Board Chairs following David Peacock: Gail Cuthbert Brandt, Principal of Canada's Rennison College; Nirmala Jeyaraj, Principal of Lady Doak College in India; and now

Michael Wright, Vice Chancellor of Canterbury Christ Church University in England. Along the way, a relabeling occurred, with AEC's replacement by CUAC as a corporate entity and the transfer of ownership of AEC's substantial financial assets in exchange for a less formal role as the American chapter of CUAC.

It has been rewarding for me to participate over the last ten years in regular AEC and CUAC gatherings in New York City and on the campuses of member institutions, both in the United States and around the world, including in Japan, England, and Hong Kong. The chief benefit of these opportunities has been the insights that presentations, conversations, and worship involving faculty, staff, students, priests, and bishops from vastly differing backgrounds have made possible. Throughout, these have been enriched by the shared traditions, theology, and liturgical forms that mark the churches of the Anglican Communion.

From time to time, participants have questioned the value of these experiences. Some have seen them as little more than an institutionally-funded Anglican travel club, and I would have to grant that there has been occasional evidence that would support that view, but my sense has been, again and again, that sharing friendship, reflection, and inspiration with colleagues from very different Anglican institutions has enriched us all and given us a greater sense of our common character than could have been achieved in any other way.

Story 6: The Lilly Endowment and Sewanee Again

The Lilly Endowment is a great American institution. Founded in 1937, through gifts from Lilly family members of stock in the Eli Lilly pharmaceutical company, to support the causes of religion, education, and community development, the Endowment has a long history of thoughtful philanthropy.

The University of the South is one of the 88 American colleges and universities that received major grants in the Endowment's Programs for the Theological Exploration of Vocation (PTEV) between 2000 and 2002. This initiative, which made grants averaging more than $2 million per institution, enabled the participating colleges and universities, many but not all of which have ties to church bodies, to develop and implement a wide variety of programs to assist students in examining the relationship between faith and vocational choices, to provide opportunities for gifted young people to explore Christian ministry, and to enhance the capacity of faculty and staff to teach and mentor students effectively in this arena. At Sewanee these programs drew together faculty and staff from broadly differing backgrounds, enriched their study and reflection in many ways including through the contributions of remarkable national and international guests, and laid the groundwork for many ongoing programs, chief of which is the Sewanee Vocational

Discernment Institute, a summer program in which Sewanee students and ones from other colleges and universities spend most of the summer in a combination of intense reflection and demanding internships in churches and other organizations engaged in service. Securing the additional endowment funds needed to support this program in future years, following the conclusion of the Lilly PTEV grant, is a high priority for my last year as Sewanee's vice chancellor.

It has been a special privilege for me to work with Council of Independent Colleges President Richard Ekman, Grinnell College President Russell Osgood, and several other leaders from PTEV and non-PTEV institutions to initiate, with generous Lilly Endowment support, a new Network for Vocation in Undergraduate Education (NetVUE), a consortium of colleges and universities committed to continuing and extending the benefits of the PTEV program.

My debt to the Lilly Endowment is a personal one as well. Over the last four years, my wife, Trudy, and I have participated in a sequence of seminars and consultations made possible by a generous Lilly grant to the Council of Independent Colleges. This program has engaged over a hundred college and university presidents and their spouses, and others who have been recognized as strong prospects to move into presidencies, in extended reading and thinking together about what we and our institutions are called to be and do. We studied and discussed many of the texts that we had read years earlier, but now with different perspectives and insights. We shared our differing interpretations of such diverse sources as the Bible, Aristotle, Toqueville, Lincoln, Bonhoeffer, Buechner, Berry, Merton, and Sayers (Schwehn and Bass; Placher). We read novels such as Pierre de Calan's *Cosmas or the Love of God* and compared our conclusions about what they said to us about our lives and our colleges. We talked about how best to care for our institutions and for ourselves, and, in particular, how best to care for our souls.

Again and again we wrestled with the tension that we have all felt between the forces of our personal ambition and our loyalty to the institutions we serve. We fought over the book *Habits of the Heart* by Robert Bellah, Richard Madsen, William Sullivan, Ann Swidler, and Steven Tipton, which makes the case that our country is losing its way because individualism is overwhelming commitments to the greater good.

Later I came on a more recent book that makes a related case. Carrying the unglamorous title *On Thinking Institutionally*, it is the work of the distinguished political scientist, Hugh Heclo, a former Harvard professor who is now Robinson Professor of Public Policy at George Mason University.

In 195 pages of engagingly crafted observation and reflection on history, politics, business, and sports, Heclo follows in the tradition of Toqueville and Bellah to make a convincing case that America is having a growing overdose of the people who are given to 'pervasive strutting, temper tantrums, trash talk, showboating, and other forms or public preening' (p. 3).

On the other hand, Heclo offers examples past and present of Americans of integrity who have been willing to sacrifice their interests to serve the common good, including George Washington, Abraham Lincoln, the whistleblowers at Enron and Worldcom, and General Antonio Taguba, who sacrificed his Army career to bring light and justice to the crimes at Abu Ghraib prison. However, Heclo concludes convincingly that the traditional values of self-sacrifice, devotion to others, and loyalty to our institutions and their rules of commitment and service are being overshadowed, and that it is not just in the famous and highly publicized that these matters are seen today. Heclo writes:

> ... in going about our daily lives we are often scandal-ized in another kind of way. For example, we encoun-ter the store attendant who is not attending to much of anything, especially the customer. Or it is the coworker who is working on everything except the task at hand. Or it might be the slacker student or the slacker teacher who is merely going through the motions of the lesson plan. What these big and little scandals all have in common amounts to this: people not doing the job that is supposed to be done (p. 108).

Heclo urges that we must somehow find our way to a better, wiser balance between the affirmation of the individual and the interests of the community. And he points out that, for many, the rewards of individual stardom are hollow and fleeting, that 'the deep satisfactions we crave come from strong bonds of mutual attachment to other people and larger causes outside ourselves' (Heclo, p. 9). In this he reaffirms a central theme of Bellah and his colleagues in *Habits of the Heart*: we need to lessen our striving to be personally number one, at whatever price to others or to our own integrity, and strengthen our commitment to the institutions that nurture us: family; church, synagogue, or mosque; and clubs and associations that serve the common good. And as Heclo puts it, the best thing most of us can do to help to bring our country into better balance is to strive to be trustworthy.

Which brings me back to Sewanee. The University of the South is an institution that has for more than 150 years successfully drawn a remarkable level of loyalty and devotion from its students, alumni, faculty, and staff. Its commitments to integrity are long and deep. In the spring of 2009, I was in court for the first time in my forty years as a university faculty member, dean, and president. I was there to defend a decision of the student-governed Honor Council of the University of the South, and as I waited for the case to be heard, I looked back over the notes I used in speaking at the University's Founders' Day Convocation in October 2008. What I said then reflects Sewanee's foundation in the Church and its commitment to the values Hugh Heclo is urging for all of us:

> Many of the problems we face in our country today are at their root problems arising from a lack of integrity. Avarice outweighed honor in decisions individuals and institutions made in seeking and granting mortgages, leading to risks that few perceived and injury that is destined to be long-lasting. The need for the education, values, and traditions that are abundant at Sewanee has never been greater.
>
> ...
>
> Recently I received a graciously autographed copy of the book *When Conscience and Power Meet,* the impressive autobiography of member of Sewanee's College Class of 1942 Eugene Ziegler. Mr. Ziegler, who has achieved distinction as a wartime naval officer, attor-

ney, legislator, and leader in the Episcopal Church, gives many examples of how his Sewanee education and friendships gave him the framework of insight and values that made possible his wholeness and success. He writes: 'I am indebted to Sewanee for planting in my mind a sense of the wholeness of life. When I graduated ... , I took with me a quotation of John Milton's that I had framed and put in my law library both to inspire me and to make me humble: 'I call therefore a complete and generous education that which fits a man to perform justly, skillfully, and magnanimously all the offices both private and public of peace and war' (p. 352).

Story 7: Scripture and Trustees

I was warned that if the Trustees elected me on Epiphany Day in 2000, as their search committee proposed, I would be expected to speak for fifteen minutes or so to accept their election. Encouraged by some of the committee members, I included in those remarks a part of the passage from the Book of Exodus in which Moses encountered the burning bush, and I told the story of the run-in Trudy and I had a few months earlier with a kind of burning bush of our own at the General Theological Seminary in New York City, a startling experience that put an end to the reservations we had had about exploring the possibility of moving to Sewanee.

The Trustees responded warmly that day, and I have included a fragment of scripture in each of my oral reports to the Trustees since then. In doing so, I realized that this ran a risk of putting off some of the audience, especially some of the unchurched members of the University community, but I reminded the occasional quibbler that Sewanee is an institution of the church and that, for churched and unchurched alike, the Bible is one of the great literary treasures of our civilization.

For reasons I have never fully understood, a few of those occasions of reporting to the Board of Trustees included moments when I felt deeply moved and tears welled up in my eyes. One such time was on Founders' Day in October 2006. The speaker at the University-wide Convocation earlier that day had been John Danforth, a highly respected former US Senator and United Nations Ambassador, Episcopal priest, wise observer of the American scene, and grandfather of a Sewanee undergraduate. Noting that the last chapter in Danforth's then-new book, *Faith and Politics*, grounds a call for grace and humility in our nation's political life on the 12th chapter of St. Paul's letter to the Romans, I recalled that when I was thirteen years old, my father had convinced me to memorize the King James version of that chapter, which after much labor, I did by the barest. As I told the Trustees, the words of that passage have not remained fully intact in my memory, but it has been a part of me ever since and has always reminded me of my father, who died two years after setting me the task of learning it. Then I read a fragment of that chapter, beginning at the tenth verse, this time from the *New Revised Standard Version*:

> Love one another with mutual affection; outdo one
> another in showing honor. Do not lag in zeal, be ardent
> in spirit, serve the Lord. Rejoice in hope, be patient in
> suffering, persevere in prayer. Contribute to the needs
> of the saints; extend hospitality to strangers.

Later I talked about some issues that were troubling and dividing us. One was a land-use feasibility study that had concerned many in Sewanee then, another was the somewhat fractious work that was underway (as outlined in Story 4 above) to express the University's purpose, and yet another was the turbulent conflict in the Episcopal Church and the Anglican Communion over whether openly gay priests should be barred from the episcopacy.

On the last of these, I reminded the Trustees of Sewanee's commitment to serve the broad whole of the Episcopal Church, even as wholeness was being tested. I said, 'unless or until you or the Regents give us other directions, we aim to give the Church the gift of being its University, a place where those from many differing points of view in the Church are in civil discourse with others, and an institution that welcomes students, faculty, and participants into its many programs, from the full range of the Church and the world.' And then I turned back to those words from St Paul, hanging especially on the admonitions to 'love one another with mutual affection' and 'extend hospitality to strangers.'

I was a bit worried that this preaching to a crowd populated heavily by bishops and priests might seem presumptuous, and it was a happy time when many thanked and encouraged me afterwards, and when one priest whom I have long admired wrote later to say that he had shared something of my remarks with his parish and that they had chosen to emphasize that fragment of scripture in reaching out to their larger community.

A Small Quilt of Reflections

It is often the case for storytellers and their listeners that the tales go on so long that there is not much time or attention left for teasing out morals or meanings, and that may be the case in this instance as well. However, I want to offer at least a few reflections.

Leaders in church-related higher education share a great deal with those who lead secular colleges and universities. An institution's being tied to a church body gives it some additional resources and constraints, but the fact that leaders successfully move back and forth between these categories makes it clear that many values and skills apply similarly in both. For example, in either setting one had better have integrity and the ability to gather support, and it is useful to be able to read a balance sheet and be resilient. In fact, it is probably true that most good counsel about leadership applies in almost all organizations, although the famed investment banker, statesman, devoted Episcopalian, and volunteer leader of many major not-for-profit organizations John C. Whitehead has written '… it is far easier to run a corporation — even a fast-moving global operation like Goldman-Sachs — than it is to run just about any nonprofit you could name'

(p. 242). The fallout from the recent turmoil in financial markets may give Mr. Whitehead some pause about this assertion, but he supports it with many examples from his own experience in which leaders of nonprofit organizations faced particular challenges in defining their missions, working with volunteers, and raising funds.

On the other hand, all colleges and universities are unique, and their needs and opportunities for leadership at any given time differ enough that observations and generalizations from some will miss the mark for others. Even so, I offer the promised small quilt of guesses and hints about leadership for colleges and universities tied to church bodies.

In early November 2009, as I was driving to the Atlanta airport for a flight to a meeting of the trustees of the Colleges and Universities of the Anglican Communion and, at the same time, thinking about how to conclude this chapter, I was also listening with half an ear to a radio interview (Gross) with the author Mary Karr, who at one point said, 'talking about spiritual activity to a secular audience is like doing card tricks on the radio.' Maybe not quite that bad, I thought, but not far off. One of the challenges for leaders of many colleges and universities with ties to religious bodies is that they need to do a good deal of that sort of talking as they work to build understanding and support for their institutions from a wide range of individuals and groups, religious and not. Many of us also have to translate and communicate in the other direction, helping church members appreciate the cautions and concerns of some faculty and others who are not in the church, often having to do with the value of academic freedom.

It is helpful to keep in mind that one is not likely to be able to please everybody in this work. Several years ago, I received reactions from two dedicated alumni to one of my *Sewanee* magazine messages. The first thanked me for having finally written one without including anything 'religious;' and the second suggested that I should have found a way in that piece to affirm the University's Episcopal character. One's goal in this regard needs to be to weave together expressions of aspiration for quality, integrity, inspiration, and service that all, or nearly all, of the members of the institution's diverse constituencies can support, but having the freedom to use the language of the faith can give a strength and soundness to the message that is envied by leaders of secular institutions.

When there is tension, conflict, or a lack of mutual respect on issues related to the institution's ties to the church, the chief contribution a leader can make is often to seek to find common ground, and remember that not all arguments need to be brought to a conclusion quickly. Personalities differ, and every leader has to be himself or herself, but in these circumstances there are clear advantages to steadiness, being at ease, and manifesting confidence in the institution and its people. Telling the right story can often yield better results than scholarly analysis. It's also a gift when the leader can manage to avoid taking offense and can give most of the credit for progress to others and take a more-than-fair share of the blame when progress does not come. It sometimes helps to remind all involved of the benefits to an academic community of courtesy, civility, and hospitality.

Leaders of higher education institutions tied to church bodies and other religious groups are often called to weave together groups and individuals with widely differing views and values. It helps if the leader is good at listening, comfortable supporting the work of others, at ease with his or her personal beliefs and ties to the religious body, and open to the possibility that someone else in the mix will come up with a better idea about how to proceed.

When a member of the search committee that is at work to find Sewanee's next vice chancellor asked me what single bit of advice I might offer my successor, the answer that tumbled out was: 'There will be times when your best efforts will be criticized severely by individuals or a group that will seem to you to be harsh, unreasonable, and unfair. Love them anyway.' As I reflected on this, I realized that this counsel not only arises from Jesus's admonition to love our neighbors as ourselves, but it is also quite practical. One of my early mentors in higher-education administration, University of Tennessee President Edward Boling, said that he learned the rule, 'Love your enemies,' at least as much from working in the Tennessee Legislature as from the Bible, since in legislative work one's enemy on one issue needs to be a friend on a future one.

Deciding how to invest our time and energy is a major challenge for most any of us, and particularly so for church-related college and university leaders. My experience is that investing in service for the church and in welcoming people with conflicting views is likely to yield much better returns than pressing one's own views on divisive issues.

A key opportunity for leaders in what this book's editors call Christian higher education is to welcome and encourage members and leaders for the future of the church and the academy. One of the obligations that I have felt strongly but will probably never fulfill adequately is to repay the gifts of my many mentors, but especially Professor George Connor, by challenging and supporting others who will lead and serve in the church and higher education in the years ahead.

There will always be tension between the ambitions of the individual leader and the interests of the institution. A few months ago I sent Hugh Heclo a copy of the notes I had used for a talk in which I had praised his book *Thinking Institutionally* that addresses that tension compellingly. His gracious response included the following: 'At the risk of seeming ungrateful, I would quibble with one point you mentioned in your talk, to the effect that I am asking people to "sacrifice their interests to serve the common good." Of course in some immediate sense that might seem true. But really, without getting into the deeper and more important things of religion, I am asking a person to think about what is good for his or her soul. That is what I was struggling to say in writing, "And while the public culture might not notice or reward these larger loyalties, they are the kinds of things we are likely to cherish when, from some terminus, we look back on the course our life has taken." I suspect you and I are both near that stage.' He is right about my stage, and I think he is right about the rest as well. In one of the Lilly-Endowment-supported gatherings of college and university presidents mentioned in story 6 above, we were asked what we most wanted our presidential legacy to be. One participant's answer helped all of us to see the question in a better light. He said, 'I hope I won't care so much how I am remembered as that the university grew stronger and more successful in serving our church in the years I served it.'

Bishop Henry Parsley, in his homily in the Eucharist of the final meeting of Sewanee's Board of Trustees just before the conclusion of his six years as Chancellor in October 2009, spoke movingly about the University, its special character as an institution of the church, and its meaning in his life. He was also more than generous in his words about Trudy and me, and he brought unexpected tears to my eyes when he remembered the talk mentioned in story 7 above. He said:

> Joel and I share a favorite passage of Scripture, the twelfth chapter of Romans, where we read, 'let love be genuine . . . hold fast to what is good ... never flag in zeal ... rejoice in your hope, be patient in tribulation, be constant in prayer. Contribute to the needs of the saints, practice hospitality.' Joel and Trudy have lived these words during their years in this office, and we salute them.

Those words, whether deserved or not, made me deeply grateful, and I thought, 'Now there's a report card that would surely have pleased my parents.'

References

Bellah, Robert N., Richard Madsen, William M. Sullivan, Ann Swidler, and Steven M. Tipton (2007), *Habits of the Heart: Individualism and Commitment in American Life*, New York: University of California.

Benne, Robert (2001), *Quality With Soul: How Six Premier Colleges and Universities Keep Faith with their Religious Traditions*, Grand Rapids: Wm. B. Eerdmans Publishing Co.

Burtchaell, James T., C.S.C. (1998), *The Dying of the Light: The Disengagement of Colleges and Universities from their Christian Churches*, Grand Rapids: Wm. B. Eerdmans Publishing Co.

Danforth, John (2006), *Faith and Politics: How the 'Moral Values' Debate Divides America and How to Move Forward Together*, New York: Penguin Group.

de Calan, Pierre (1980), *Cosmas, or, The Love of God*, Translated from French by Peter Hebblethwaite, London: Collins.

Edwards, Mark U. (2006), *Religion on our Campuses: A Professor's Guide to the Communities, Conflicts, and Promising Conversations*, New York: Palgrave Macmillan.

Gardner, John William (1990), *On Leadership*, New York: Free Press.

Gross, Terry, interviewer (2009), *Fresh Air from WHYY: NPR*, Philadelphia: WHYY Radio, November 3, 2009 (Audio).

Hart, Jeffrey (2001), *Smiling Through the Cultural Catastrophe: Toward the Revival of Higher Education*, New Haven: Yale University Press.

Heclo, Hugh (2008), *On Thinking Institutionally*, Boulder: Paradigm.

Hughes, Richard T. (2005), *The Vocation of a Christian Scholar: How Christian Faith Can Sustain the Life of the Mind*, Grand Rapids: Wm. B Eerdmans Publishing Co.

Hughes, Richard T. and William B. Adrian, ed. (1997), *Models for Christian Higher Education: Strategies for Success in the 21st Century*, Grand Rapids: Wm. B. Eerdmans Publishing Co.

Jacobsen, Douglas, Rhonda H. Jacobsen, and Martin E. Marty (2004), *Scholarship & Christian Faith: Enlarging the Conversation*, New York: Oxford University Press.

Placher, William C., ed. (2006), *Callings: Twenty Centuries of Christian Wisdom on Vocation*. Grand Rapids: Wm. B. Eerdmans Publishing Co.

Schwehn, Mark R. (1993), *Exiles from Eden: Religion and the Academic Vocation in America*, New York: Oxford University Press.

Schwehn, Mark R. and Dorothy C. Bass, ed. (2006), *Leading Lives that Matter: What We Should Do and Who We Should Be*, Grand Rapids: Wm. B. Eerdmans Publishing Co.

Sittler, Joseph (1986), *Gravity and Grace: Reflections and Provocations*, Minneapolis: Augsburg Publishing House.

Whitehead, John C. (2005), *A Life in Leadership: From D-Day to Ground Zero*, New York: Basic Books.

Williamson, Samuel R., Jr. (2008), *Sewanee Sesquicentennial History: The Making of the University of the South*, Sewanee: The University of the South.

Ziegler, Eugene N. (2008), *When Conscience and Power Meet: A Memoir*, Columbia: The University of South Carolina Press.

Nirmala Jeyaraj

Christian Higher Education in India

Contemporary Challenges for Leadership

As part of the globalization process, our modern society is undergoing rapid transformation in all domains including politics, economics, technology, education, religion and culture. Current economic crisis and the on-going environmental catastrophe due to climate change are global threats that call for the immediate attention of all countries to promote equitable and sustainable development through co-operative action. Technology has thrown open immense opportunities for individual and societal development. There is a worldwide knowledge revolution. Knowledge itself is becoming a new powerful global product. Alvin Toffler discusses the transforming power shift in our human society from the industrial past to the knowledge-based future in his book Power Shift (1990, pp. 3–20). Information technology and communicative English are given prime importance in education at all levels. With the great leaps in information, media and communication technology and efficient transport facilities, the global society is becoming more complex. While multiculturalism and religious pluralism are becoming widespread, there is also the danger of overshadowing or disappearance of indigenous cultures by the dominant culture of the West.

The impact of globalization on education is significant. Economy is knowledge based and education has become commercialized, privatized and capitalized. These days it is becoming more a marketable commodity for profit making than a noble service. In the context of increased competitiveness and internationalization of higher education, Christian institutions are challenged to respond to the market forces for survival without compromising on Christian values. This calls for a reflection on their Christian mission in relation to the changing society.

I have discussed various issues of leadership in Christian Higher Education in different forums and in my papers presented in consultations in India and abroad.[1] In this paper, I have tried to bring out the relevance and significance of Christian higher education in the current context, tracing its history, objectives and impact on the Indian society. I have elaborated on the challenges for Christian leadership in higher education and the responses to those challenges keeping to the Christian ideals and mission. Further, 'Christian identity' of our church or mission institutions is explained

1   Refer to my paper 'Developing Women Leadership in Colleges' presented at the 3rd International Conference of CUAC held at Trinity College, Toronto, 1999 and 'Servant Leadeship and Organizational Culture' presented at the Consultation of CUAC-India Chapter held on 10th Nov 2007 at Isabella Thoburn College, Lucknow.

and 'Christian presence' in our campuses and curriculum is clarified in relation to the fast changing globalized society. This leads to the question on the nature of leadership that is required in Christian higher education institutions. The leadership is challenged to restructure the educational system and lay down appropriate policies and processes in place to promote relevance, inclusiveness, equity and excellence while keeping the Christian foundation strong. Commitment to Gospel values, contextualization and developing competence to excel would make Christian leadership distinctive. Examples are sited from my 12 years of experience in educational leadership as Principal and Secretary of Lady Doak College, a premier Women's Christian institution in Madurai, South India. My leadership in the Executive Board of Colleges and Universities of Anglican Communion (CUAC) as a member (3 terms) and as the Chair (one term), as Vice President in All India Association of Christian Higher Education (AIACHE), as a Syndicate Member in the Madurai Kamaraj University and as member in the Governing Boards of several colleges in the region has provided me ample opportunities to learn sound leadership principles and practices. I very much hope that my sharing in this paper would be useful to those Principals/ Presidents who are leading mission founded institutions in a secular, multi-faith and globalised society.

Origin and Development of Higher Education in India

Education in ancient India was non-formal to begin with. Families and communities passed on their knowledge, skill and experience to the next generation mainly by oral traditions. Later, during the Vedic period, the 'Gurukula Model' of learning was developed particularly to study Vedas, but this was restricted to upper castes particularly Brahmins. On the contrary, Buddhism through their 'Monastry Model' of education opened education to anyone interested irrespective of caste, creed or sex. For example, Nalanda and Taksasila, ancient centers of learning that were equivalent to universities offered teachings in the fields of sacred and secular, philosophical and practical, science and arts, attracting scholars even from overseas (Jeyaraj, 2004).

In the medieval period, education emphasized more on learning of religious scriptures than common knowledge. The missionaries from Europe particularly Britain, Germany, Denmark and Sweden and North America started their educational mission establishing schools and colleges in different parts of the country to reach out people from all strata of society. The earliest formal Christian educational institution was Francis Xavier's St. Paul's College of 1540 in Goa (Augustine, 2006, p. 17). Missionaries belonging to the Western churches and missions started a number of Christian schools during 17th to 19th centuries in different parts of the country.

The higher education system in India dates back to 1782 when Lord Warren Hastings founded the Calcutta Madrasa. The establishment of Hindu College in 1817 followed this. The Wood's Dispatch in 1854 led to the development of three universities (Government sponsored) after the pattern of London University, in the major cities of India, namely Calcutta, Bombay and Madras. Later Punjab University in 1882 and Allahabad University in 1887 were established. All the five universities were mere affiliating bodies and had no direct teaching until the University Commission in 1902 re-organized them as teaching bodies setting rules for governance and affiliation (Aggarwall 2003, pp. 98–100). The educational policy laid in 1904 brought in the 'grant-in-aid system' for schools and colleges. Unfortunately, the world's third largest system of higher education as that of India follows both the affiliating and grant-in-aid model till date while the West from where it originated is limiting or gradually removing it.

The Serampore Trio, William Carey, Marshman and Ward established the country's first Christian college in the outskirts of Calcutta in 1818. Other landmark institutions that were established later by missionaries were St. Stephen's College, Delhi by the Cambridge Mission, Wilson College at Bombay and the Madras Christian College at Chennai. While the Christian higher education expanded fast, there was a demand for government funded non-missionary education. There was a steady growth in higher education from the latter half of 19th century and this trend continued in the 20th century even after Independence. During the first half of 20th century, secondary and higher education increased twenty fold in terms of number of schools, colleges and universities and a sizable fraction of these were Christian institutions (Aggarwal, 2003).

Though government sponsored non-missionary education started growing significantly, it was catering more to the rich and upper classes of the society whereas the missionary education reached out to the masses particularly the poor and lower castes. For example, the converted mass in South India from among the lower castes found new opportunities to prosper through education provided by Christian mission institutions (Ingleby, 2000, pp. 1–15).

Other than the Christian missionary educational model, during the period of struggle for independence, Gandhi developed an alternative model of education of masses more of a non-formal type, without neglect of basic education. His 'Ashram Model' focused on the community as a whole. Similarly, Rabindranath Tagore started a school at Shantiniketan that grew into a world university called 'Visvabharti', following Gandhi's philosophy integrating harmonious living with nature. However, only the 'University Model' of the West developed by the British became widely accepted and practiced till date at the national level.

After Independence, most of the missions gradually withdrew leaving their institutions under Indian leadership to be managed by churches or by independent boards. At present, the Christian institutions constitute only about 2–3% of the largely expanded system of Indian Higher Education. Yet there is a tremendous scope to influence the modern society acting like a pinch of salt.

Higher Education of women

Having the passion, commitment and experience in promoting higher education of women and having been associated with a women's college for nearly four decades, I wish to focus on the development and significance of women's education in India particularly highlighting the contribution of missionaries.

Women in ancient India enjoyed an honorable status equal to men. They were well educated and played a significant role in the cultural, economic, political, religious and social life as evidenced in Vedas (Vijayalakshmi, 2005, pp. 103–113). It was only during the Hindu Manu's time by 100 AD women were pushed down to a lower dependent status, exploited, subjugated and oppressed, with the denial of access to education and public life. Their dignity and freedom as individuals were taken away and women were considered as mere property of men (father, husband and son) from birth to death. Under the patriarchal system, Indian prejudices against the education of women were strong and deep. It was the Christian missionaries during the 19th century who opened the doors of formal education to women and inspired social reformation. Indian reformers like Raja Ram Mohan Roy, Vidyasagar and Pandita Ramabai fought the evil practices against women such as Sati, female infanticide, Purdah system, Devadasi practice and child marriage and strongly advocated widow's remarriage and education of girls. This led to the founding of schools for women in different states of India and the nation could witness a tremendous expansion in the field of women's education. The literacy of women increased from 0.5 in 1881 to 40% by 1991.

Moving to higher education of women, initially, the doors of universities were closed for girls until 1877, when Calcutta University for the first time permitted women to appear for examinations. Subsequently other universities in Madras and Bombay also opened the doors for women. Provision was made for professional education in 1883 by admitting women in Medical College. In the South, Dr. Ida Scudder started the Christian Medical College (CMC) at Vellore in 1900 to train women professionally as doctors and nurses. Maharishi Anna Sahib Karve established SNDT Women's University as the first women's University in 1916 on the model of Japanese Women's University (Pillai 1998).

Several missionaries from different mission organizations and churches pioneered women's higher education across the country. Lucknow Women's college was the first women's college in Asia, that was founded in 1886 by Isabella Thoburn, an American missionary, sponsored by the Women's Society of the Methodist Church. Initially affiliated to Calcutta University, it was later shifted to Allahabad University and was renamed after the founder since her death in 1901. Church Mission Society established Sarah Tucker College in Tirunelveli, located in South Tamil Nadu Nadu as the first women's college in South India in 1895 to train women as teachers. Many other women's colleges were subsequently established: Women's Christian College in Madras founded by Dr Eleanor McDougall in1915 as a joint venture of 12 missionary societies; Kinnaird College for women in Lahore by Zenana and Bible Medical Mission in

1913; Lady Doak College in 1948 founded by Dr. Katie Wilcox of American Board of Congregational Churches. These are some of the leading institutions known for their outstanding educational service and quality even until date.

Mission and Goal of Christian Higher Education ...then and now

I wish to first touch upon the basis and goals of early missionary educational enterprise in India and many have debated this at length. The basis of educational enterprise in India by Christian community was its commitment to impart knowledge and to leaven society with values based on the life and teachings of Jesus Christ (Augustine, 2006, pp. 17–35). The church and missionary societies initially began educational mission for evangelization and to train the work force for church and civil services. Nevertheless, it has served beyond doubt a 'social uplift' for the culturally and economically deprived communities and a civilizing purpose overall (Desrochers, 1998, pp. 149–56). Over the centuries, there has been diverse missionary thinking and their plans and purposes have been changing according to the context. Caldwell School founded in a village in South Tamil Nadu offered education in vernacular medium and were effective in civilizing a backward populace. Secondary and higher education in English medium like that of Anderson & Miller in Madras city catered to the high caste Hindus providing moral standards, feeding the hungry minds, introducing useful ideas and in general promoting the cause of Christian civilization, thus proving the 'Diffusion Theory' (Ingleby, 2000, pp. 361–79). However, missionary education was blamed to promote cultural imperialism, family centeredness, clan and community affinity remained strong and unfortunately, caste discrimination prevails as the greatest evil in Indian society, practiced till date even among the Indian Christians. Another point to note is, in spite of tremendous expansion of missionary education during the later part of 19th century and beyond, conversion to Christianity had been minimal as evidenced by the Christian population staying at 2–3%.

Today, largely Christian institutions enjoy a respectable status and are well recognized by the Government agencies as well as the public for quality, excellence, values and service. But they are being challenged by the forces of globalization and are in need of leadership with missionary vision and zeal. It is the responsibility of the leadership to sustain and promote quality and credibility, preserving the reputation of Christian institutions. In the present context, churches, educators and leaders of Christian institutions should first have the conviction that it is part of *Christian responsibility, Christian service and Christian witness* to be engaged in the educational endeavor in a country like India where only about 10% of the age group is in higher education unlike other developing countries. Secondly, they should identify with the goal of Christian Higher Education in general and the mission of their own institution in particular. I recall the statement of Dr M.A. Thangaraj, on the goal of Christian Higher education i.e. 'to produce intellectually mature, morally upright, socially responsible and spiritually inspired young men and women to serve the society'.[2] Many Chris-

---

2   M. A. Thangaraj's paper presented at the Conference for Christian Colleges held at ECC, Whitefiled in1993 sponsored by UBCHE.A

tian colleges have incorporated this in their mission statement and this is very well applicable to all institutions.
Identifying with the mission and goal of the institution gives
a strong footing to the institutional leadership.

Current scenario of Indian Higher Education-
Challenges and Responses of Christian Leadership

Expansion, Inclusion and Equity

Let me elaborate on the status of higher education with particular reference to Christian colleges and universities. The
higher education system of India has seen twenty five-fold
increase in the number of universities (including Deemed
Universities) and 35-fold increase in the number of colleges
in comparison to the number at the time of Independence
(Sharma and Neeraj Kaushik, 2007). During the last two
decades, the number of universities and research institutes,
Arts and Science colleges, teacher-training colleges and medical colleges has doubled, while the number of engineering
colleges has disproportionately increased fivefold. The overall enrolment of women students in higher education has significantly increased to 40%, but with only 12–15% enrolment
in professional courses and still not on par with men enrolment (Jacob, 2007). There are many men's colleges, which
have become co-educational recently, but colleges exclusively for women continue to function, catering to those who
prefer exclusive women's institutions.

There is a mushrooming of educational institutions, particularly engineering and teacher training colleges initiated mostly by private individuals or trusts. A large majority of them has profit making as their motive and serves the middle and upper classes of the society. These self-financed institutions do not get the support of the grant-in-aid system and as such, pay poor salary to teachers in spite of charging exorbitantly high fees and in addition collecting capitation fees, the rate varying based on the demand for the courses. Meritorious or non-meritorious but economically well-off students are able join paying the capitation and other fees, whereas students from deprived socio-economic background and marginalized communities get excluded and are not able to get into courses with good job prospects. Recognizing this exclusion, the government has prioritized inclusive education in its 11th Five Year development plan and the University Grants Commission has proposed to start new universities with government funding in the rural areas particularly to make higher education accessible to the rural poor. The national vision for 2020 is to enhance the percentage of relevant age group in tertiary education from the current 10% to above 20% level as in other developing countries. What contribution could the Christian managements and churches make in expanding Higher Education and making it inclusive?

Today many Christian institutions are among the top ranking ones and are appreciated for their quality and educational service. Having the rich heritage of the missionary legacy and enjoying the privileges provided in our Constitution for minorities, they are at a much advantageous position. However, the question here is whom are they serving? Who are the beneficiaries? Many of the Christian organizations have joined the bandwagon of profit making institutions charging high fees and as 'elitists' serve the 'haves' and are not concerned about those at the bottom rung in the society. I see a clear cut mandate here for Christian managements and churches. It is their responsibility to provide higher educational opportunities to the disadvantaged sections of the society such as women, scheduled castes, scheduled tribes and other educationally and economically backward communities irrespective of their religious affiliation, as done by missionaries of earlier centuries. Walking the extra mile to uplift the poor and marginalized through empowering education would involve viz.:

(a) At entry level—lowering off the merit line for admission, giving additional training to prospective students to upgrade their standards as required for entry (something similar to a bridge course given before entry), adapting reservation policies that is not just community based as stipulated by the government; instead use a discriminative index that is based on socio-economic factors such as family income, family size, locality of the school- rural or urban, medium of instruction, education of parents etc; provide free tuition & scholarships and residential facilities

(b) During the course of study—extend additional help such as extra tutoring, coaching and peer learning to enable successful graduation

(c) Prior or after graduation—provide career guidance, training and facilitate placement or to develop as entrepreneurs. All these would enhance access and make Christian higher education **'inclusive'** provided the leadership has the compassion and commitment to implement these initiatives. Such steps would definitely pave the way for building an equitable society.

Liberal arts curriculum and Alternate models of education

Another concern of Indian higher education is the lopsided growth of professional education with the demand for Liberal Arts education and Basic Sciences diminishing day by day. Undue importance is given to Information Technology and option of courses by the parents as well as students is based on the salary package they would earn after graduation. Liberal Arts colleges are struggling to fill the seats in some of their courses. The leaders and educational experts need to develop innovative curriculum for integrated and holistic learning. Moreover, there is a great mismatch between the human resource produced and what is needed in the job market. The challenge is to bring relevance and utility in higher education while integrating Liberal Arts curriculum with professional education, technical skills with soft skills and holistic development with expertise in highly specialized fields. These have to be creatively addressed by leaders in Christian education.

Another option the Christian institutional leaders may consider is to devise and implement alternate modes of education such as open or distance learning and innovative educational programs such as **Community Colleges**, deviating from the traditional model. The target population again would be the school dropouts and others in the age group who have no means to enter the portals of higher education but who are in need of education for life and livelihood. They may be from the urban and rural poor communities. The Western model of 'Community Colleges' has been adopted after suitable modification based on the Indian context and the Catholic Missions are taking a lead in this. Other Christian managements running educational institutions may also initiate special education programs through such Community Colleges and expand higher education to reach out to the needy.

This leads to the question of finance to run these community colleges. The target group may need a heavy subsidy apart from the initial investment for infrastructure and maintenance. Both the churches and Christian educational institutions have under their possession huge properties, lands and infrastructure inherited from the missions. Sadly, there are instances of even selling some of these mission properties for personal gain by either church authorities or individuals in charge of property maintenance with no integrity or accountability. Instead, if they could make an investment in income generating projects and the profit could be used to provide subsidized education for the marginalized, it would justify the goal of earlier mission. Moreover, well reputed Christian colleges and universities run self-financed courses that generate reasonable income. If at least 20–30% of the profit could be set apart for supporting the education of the marginalized, that would be in line with the Gospel values.

Another question I wish to raise here is, should Christian institutions focus on promoting equity or excellence, since these two counteract in certain ways. The answer is both the goals should be pursued simultaneously. This is a challenge to the leaders of Christian institutions. How to balance equity and excellence? Any institution could be an excellent institution. What makes Christian institutions different from the rest is that they not only pursue excellence but also take conscious efforts to achieve equity. For example, when admissions are made, it is not based on merit alone but other socio-economic factors have to be taken into consideration such as first generation learners, students from rural background, difficult family circumstance and so on. Such preferential option when exercised may require some lenience on the requirement of merit for admission. One cannot argue that this would lower the standards and quality of education. In order to set right the imbalance in the social set up, such preferential option or positive discrimination is required and is justifiable since it promotes equity. Thus, the issues of expansion, inclusiveness, equity and excellence are all interconnected and have to be understood and dealt with in a holistic manner by Christian educators.

Quality Assessment and Accreditation

Quality consciousness has become visible in the Indian Higher education system during the last two decades and National Assessment and Accreditation Council (NAAC), an arm of University Grants Commission has been set to assess and accredit colleges and universities in India. This has contributed to a significant improvement in the quality of Indian

Higher Education. NAAC has formulated a value-framework that provides a broad vision of higher education in developing countries in general and India in particular. The five core values stated are- contribution to nation building, promotion of global competencies, inculcation of human values, Information and Communication Technology (ICT) enabled teaching, learning and administration and above all a quest for excellence. These core principles align well with the goals of Christian higher education. In fact, many of the Christian colleges in the country have emerged as top ranking institutions in the accreditation process of NAAC. The next step is to go for international accreditation so that they could compete at global level to attract students. It would also favor international exchange and collaboration with foreign universities. Unless the leaders of Christian Colleges and Universities take ample, measure for continuous up gradation of facilities and curriculum and offer relevant and innovative academic programs they would be left behind in the race.

Christian Presence

Christian presence in higher education is the expression of Christian values in the curriculum and campus life. It is not just conducting worship services at the college chapel every day, saying Christian prayers at all functions and organizing various Christian studies programs and activities. These are important particularly to nurture Christian formation and develop the students from various Christian denominational backgrounds who constitute about 10 to 50% of the student population in Christian institutions. The percentage of Christian students in our campuses varies in the different regions of the country. But the rest of the student population and a sizable proportion of staff and faculty are from non-Christian (Hindu, Islam, Jain, Parsee, Sikh and other religious and secular) background. It would be a Christian witness if our institutional mission, ethos, organizational culture, traditions and practices are centered around the core values of the Gospel and are reflected in the various programs of our institutions- curricular, co-curricular, extra-curricular, extension, all other off-campus and on-campus activities and in the entire functioning of the institution. Such a curriculum would influence the young students to imbibe Christian values.

Christian values in today's multi-faith, multicultural society are articulated broadly as humane values namely, justice, equality, peace, reconciliation, tolerance, forgiveness, gender equity, inclusivity, inter-national and inter-religious understanding, support of the least advantaged, care for the environment and so on. In essence, it is the harmonious living with the Creator God, His creation, the humans and other living and non-living components of this World Ecosystem. Leaders and managers of Christian Higher Education are called to creatively integrate these values into their educational programs and institutional practices.

Let me site how some of these values were integrated into the curriculum at Lady Doak College. In addition to integrating these values into the content and pedagogy of regular disciplines wherever possible, a few academic centers such as the center for environmental studies, center for women's studies, center for interfaith relations and Human rights unit were initiated to break the barriers between the traditional academic subjects and foster a trans-disciplinary or integrated approach to the study of environment, gender, human rights and such other emerging areas. Interested faculty members from different disciplines get together to plan, implement and co-ordinate the curricular, extracurricular, research, extension and community outreach activities. The innovative pedagogy adopted in teaching these courses are found to have a liberating and transforming influence on the students and the community.

Christian Identity

Having elaborated on 'Christian presence' in higher education, I wish to focus on Christian identity. In other words, what are some of the attributes or qualities that distinguish Christian Higher Education Institutions? Dr. Felix Wilfred (2002), in his address at the Asian Christian faculty fellowship held in Thailand, lists several criteria to identify the Christian character of our institutions.

1. *Cultivation of quality human relationships* between the teacher and the taught and others engaged in the learning process and promoting personal attention, care and concern.

2. *Democratic and participatory practices* — globalization subtly erodes democracy through the disguise of 'management' and Christian institutions should be careful in following the principles, processes of democracy, and reflect the spirit of participation at every level. It will be easy for the leader to run our institutions with no

consultation, dialogue and participation of the staff and students in decision making. Nevertheless, let us not yield to such temptations under the pressure of globalization.

3.   *Respect for human dignity and rights* — Human rights are violated in the name of success, efficiency and profit. Christian institutions should uphold the dignity and value of every human being irrespective of their age, gender, caste, creed, color, socio-economic status, etc. and not violate the right of anyone.

4.   *Promotion of harmony and peace* — Today in the Indian, Asian and World context, there is an urgent need to discourage religious fundamentalism and promote interfaith understanding and dialogue so that there would be mutual respect and tolerance. While our institutions are strongly rooted in Christian principles and ideals, the Christian identity should be reflected more in practice than in preaching. We need to provide the right training for harmonious living and peaceful co-existence of different religious traditions.

5.   *Resisting spread of individualism through strengthening community orientation* — Autonomy of the person is a positive value while individualism is not. Globalization with its economic agenda promotes individualism and we do not want our institutions to nurture our students as self-seeking individuals. The leaders need to take enough care to train them to focus on the need of others.

6. *Socially and politically conscious education* — Globalization seems to anesthetize the social consciousness of people. The students graduating out of our campuses may have brilliant academic records, but if they lack social and political awareness, we will be failing in our duty in shaping the younger generation for responsible citizenship. Christian educators have the obligation to instill a critical sense about society and awaken their social conscience.

7. *Privileging the last and the least* — I have already elaborated in the earlier section of this chapter on equity and inclusiveness and we have the missionary model from our own history. The Christian character should be seen today in our ability to create leaders out of the underprivileged.

The above seven criteria may be used as a checklist for confirming the 'Christian identity' of our institutions. Continuous re-engineering of our institutional programs and practices to demonstrate Christian identity should be the priority for the institutional leaders in this fast changing times

Personal Leadership Attributes

In this last section, I wish to share some of the leadership qualities and practices that I found useful in my leadership career. I am not a management expert to discuss the theories of leadership and what I share here is what I have learnt from my experience.

In a higher education set up, though there is a CEO, the leadership is that of a flat organizational characteristic and is participatory. The administrators, faculty, staff, student leaders, parents most often share the responsibility with other stake holders involved in the education process. The decision making process may be slowed down and prove difficult to arrive at consensus. However, it is worth since it aligns with the democratic and Christian principles. Further, it necessitates adequate leadership training to be given at all levels and this the top leadership should facilitate. In my experience, I found sharing of responsibilities and authorities results in empowering all involved and this makes the institution stronger.

The personal goal of the leader should be to fulfill God's call and to glorify Him rather than for personal gain- monetary or name and fame. There is always the temptation to seek man's praise, but Jesus' 'servant leadership model' should be our reference.

In leadership, there is a temptation to become task oriented than people oriented. In an educational set up involving human resource development, individuals need to be cared for, respected and their needs considered. Abuse of power and position for revengeful action would be totally non-Christian and prove detrimental to the progress of the institution. People would get de-motivated and their contribution to the institutional development would be minimized. It is a challenge for the leaders to strike a balance between institutional interest and individual needs.

One of the leadership tips that I learnt as a leader is to focus on the positive side of persons, identify their strengths and provide them opportunities to use their strengths to benefit the institution. When they perform well enabled by the support of the leadership, they need to be appreciated and recognized. This serves as an encouragement to enhance their motivation level and improve performance in future. Eventually they develop as leaders and support the growing institution like the branches of a Banyan tree. Instead, if one focuses on the weakness of an individual, it brings irritation, frustration, and certain amount of bias against the person. Let us keep in mind the transforming leadership model of Jesus. The disciples were very ordinary people with their own limitations but Jesus was able to work with them and transform them so that they could carry on His mission after He left this earth.

One of the advantages of being in education is that both the teacher and the taught grow simultaneously so also the leader. One feels young, energized and refreshed in being and working among the youth imparting education.

One final question, who should lead Christian Institutions? What should be their religious identity? Unlike the Church universities in UK, Christian colleges and universities in India are mostly headed as Principals or Presidents who are qualified laypersons. Nevertheless, membership in Governing bodies consists of church leaders, educationists, business people and others from Christian denominations as specified by the Indian Constitution for Minority Rights, which has provision for establishing educational institutions and administering them exclusively by Christians. What is more important here is the leader of Christian institutions should not only be a professing Christian but also a practicing Christian combining faith and action. The faculty composition is generally mixed and so the students. Christian institutions have the responsibility to serve the Christians as well as those belonging to other faiths and therefore this composition is justifiable.

Sometimes there is tension developing between the church and institutional leadership on ownership and management issues. Churches try to take total control of educational institutions and interfere with their functioning. This has to be sorted out carefully without impinging on the right of each other but fostering cordial and synergic relationship between church and institution.[3]

Concluding Comment

To summarize, Christian higher education is education of the head, heart and hand. It is liberating in the sense that it opens the eyes of the learners bringing awareness of self and society. It is transformative to effect changes in values, attitudes and behavior of the learner, which in turn transform the society. It is also empowering the learner with knowledge, skills, critical and analytical thinking so that they move out of the

---

3   Refer to my paper 'Churches and Educational Institutions- Engaging in fruitful Partnership 'presented at the 6th CUAC 6th Triennial Conference held at Chung Chi College, Hong Kong in 2009 discusses this issue of Church-Institution partnership at length.

culture of silence to self-expression and self-assertion and act as catalytic agents to bring the desired changes in the society. To put it in a nutshell, Christian higher education is to educate human beings for fullness of life and this requires a leadership that reflects the life and teaching of Jesus Christ and responds to challenges creatively and proactively. I very much wish and hope that Christian higher Educational institutions would continue to function as torchbearers to lead others in the path of progress and fulfillment of purpose.

References

Aggarwal, J.C. (2003), *Modern Indian Education: History, Development and Problems*, Delhi: Shipla Publications.

Augustine, Mithra G. (2006), *The Second Mile*, Bangalore: Word Makers P. Ltd.

Desrochers, John (1998), *Education for Social Change*, Bangalore: CSA.

Ingleby, J.C. (2000), *Missionaries, Education and India :Issues in Protestant Missionary Education in the Long Nineteenth Century*, Delhi: ISPCK.

Jacob, Mani (2007), 'Equity vis-à-vis Quality in Higher Education: A Challenge for Christian Colleges in India' — a paper presented at the Conference of CUAC-India Chapter held at Bishop Heber College, Trichy.

Jeyaraj, J.B. (2004), 'Higher Education, Models and Value Orientation' in *New Frontiers in Education* (NFE), New Delhi: AiACHE, Vol. 34, 2, pp. 107–14. (Also republished in *Education and Mission*, Bangalore: TBT, 2007, pp. 148–61.)

Pillai, J. Kothai (1998), 'Development of Women's Education' in *Higher Education: Vision and Mission for 21st Century* (ed. Nirmala Jeyaraj), Madurai: LDC, pp. 28–61.

Sharma, Anita and Neeraj Kaushik (2007), 'Higher Education in India: Challenges Ahead' in *Higher Education in India*, Hyderabad: ICFAI University Pres.

Toeffler, Alvin (1990), *Power Shift*, New York: Bantam Book.

Vijayalakshmi, M.N. (2005), 'Women's Movement in India' in *Women and Society* (ed. Nirmala Jeyaraj), Delhi: ISPCK.

Wilfred, Felix (2002), 'Rethinking Christian Identity in Global Process'—a paper presented at the Asian Christian Faculty Fellowship held at Payap University, Thailand.

Jeremy Law

A Distinctive Vocation

Serving the Economy of Life[1]

Introduction

What, if anything, makes a Church Higher Education Institution (HEI) a *Church* HEI? This question of distinctiveness, as it is commonly understood, would appear to have been the permanent 'examination question' faced by every major report on British Church Colleges and Universities during the last twenty years. *150 Years: The Church Colleges in Higher Education* (1989), *An Excellent Enterprise* (1994), *The Way Ahead* (2001), *Mutual Expectations* (2006) and most recently *A Guide to Governance* (2007) have each, in their various ways, sought to find an answer. The repeated addressing of the

---

1 This chapter constitutes an expanded version of a paper given at the inaugural conference of the British Chapter of CUAC at the Institute of Education, London University, on May 27 2009.

question, however, suggests that no one response has been entirely adequate. At one level this is not surprising, indeed is as it should be, for to seek an answer to this question is to engage in contextual theology. It is to search for a theological account of education suited to its peculiar place and time. Yet, at another level, the repeated attempts at an answer engender a certain nervousness, a queasy feeling that perhaps every attempt is aimed at shoring up an edifice that is in an inevitable sate of collapse. Each attempt seeks to hold the line a little further down the hill until gravity claims its final victory.

This chapter, then, could be read as just one more attempt to stabilise the edifice, to halt the unstoppable trend towards 'secularisation' and the reaching of an end point where the only distinction between a Church HEI and any other is a question of historical origin, not present practice. The argument presented here is not, however, born of a defensive intention. It arises rather from the conviction that an opportune moment has arisen when the affirmation of the distinctive identity of Church HEIs will serve not simply the narrow interests of their own niche, but contribute to the common good of Higher Education. Today what began as tiny church colleges for teacher training are taking their place as major contributors to Higher Education. And, as most of them become universities in their own right, transmuted in size and scope beyond the wildest imaginings of their founders, they have the potential to re-nourish the vision of the purpose of a university precisely from the Christian tradition of their founding. Why? Well because, to put it bluntly, a university worthy of the name is essentially a theological entity concerned with the ambition of discerning what counts as reality. At a time when Higher Education is increasingly being chained to the utilitarian end of serving the interests of the national economy[2], it is worth recalling the vocation of the university to reach out beyond the given and the immediate, and that of instrumental value, towards a critical understanding of what is true[3]. The presence of the Gospel of Jesus Christ within Church HEIs, properly and appropriately conceived, is what gives them grounds to challenge the educational status quo.

A 'Reality Check'

Before proceeding further, it will be helpful to clarify what are and are not realistic expectations of an existing Church HEI. To this end, Adrian Thatcher (2004) offers us an honest and cautious word. The *Engaging the Curriculum* programme, of which Adrian Thatcher was the Director, was a modest and wholly worthy attempt to affirm that, if the distinctiveness of the Church Colleges (as they then were) meant anything tangible, then it meant a distinctive curriculum rather than, say, a reference to an inchoate notion of ethos. As such

---

2   This was one of the observations of 'A Church of England Contribution to Thinking About a Framework for Higher Education', offered by the Board of Education in 2009.

3   For a pertinent account of how such apparently contrasting figures as John Henry Newman and Jacques Derrida can contribute to a notion of the University as essentially unconditioned, and so relating to the divine, see Gerard Loughlin (2004).

it was the great hope of *An Excellent Enterprise* (1994: 130–31). Yet, writing in 2004, Thatcher affirms the general consensus that it has been a failure; it had aroused suspicion, fear and at best indifference, instead of its intended aim of allowing insights from the Christian tradition to contribute to learning as one voice among many. From this failure Thatcher draws a stark conclusion:

> [*Engaging the Curriculum*] showed that the [Church Colleges] were already post-religious, indeed deeply secular, and even fearful of acknowledging their religious roots ... If the term 'Christian university' implies a Christian curriculum, the [Church Colleges] will not be able to oblige. (Thatcher, 2004: 171)

Church HEIs are not, and could not easily become, theological colleges writ large. They are not places where it is reasonable to assume a broadly-shared understanding of the validity of the Christian tradition, one that also manifests itself in common worship and consensual pursuit of the virtues. The process of expansion (which has on occasion included merger with a 'secular' institution) has rendered this vision untenable. Moreover, the path to university status, on the part of the Church Colleges, has coincided with a period of extraordinary levels of Government control on the shape of an institution by a process of multiple quality audits. Thus if the present Church HEI's escaped colonisation by a university *from without* (such as befell St Luke's College, Exeter), still there has been a significant degree of colonisation by the essentially 'secular' university which has grown *from within* under external encouragement.

Yet the Church HEIs, as a distinct species, have not disappeared. Instead they have demonstrated a remarkable resilience for maintaining the desire that the 'faith distinctive', as *A Guide to Governance* (2007) has it, should mean something. The very fact that the question of distinctiveness is still one to be worried over, at least by Governing Bodies, Heads of Institution, Senior Management Teams and chaplains, is indicative of an abiding aspiration for its enactment. The breadth of attendance at the recent inaugural conference of the British Chapter of CUAC (Colleges and Universities of the Anglican Communion)[4] also suggests the continuing currency of this concern. To these voices must be added the often silent witness of those for whom the signs of church foundation, such as a prominent Chapel used regularly for worship, hold a representative significance, so making many positively disposed towards the church identity of their institution even in the absence of any active, personal commitment to Christianity[5]. At the very least, then, there exists a persistent appetite for discovering how Church HEIs can meaningfully enact their identity. It is as a contribution to the encouragement of that appetite that this chapter is conceived.

4   May 27 2009.
5   See Leslie Francis (2004). This work is based on empirical data from the mid 1990s, and so may not accurately reflect the present. It also focussed on students, not staff. The results do resonate, however, with recent personal experience on the part of the author concerning both staff and students.

The Privatisation of Faith

In *Nature, Man and God* (1935) William Temple, later Arch-bishop of Canterbury, allowed himself the speculative question: What was the most disastrous moment in European history? His answer took him to the winter of 1619–20 and the day René Descartes closeted himself in a small room warmed by a stove in order to strive for the rock-certain foundation upon which, like a mathematical proof, a secure understanding of the world could be erected.[6] His method was one of 'hyperbolical doubt'. He resolved '... never to accept anything as true if I did not know clearly that it was so ... that I had no opportunity to cast doubt on it' (Descartes, 1999: 16).

By degrees he sought to remove from his mind anything over which it was possible to have the slightest doubt. Perhaps what he took to be reality was only a dream. Thus he must doubt the existence of the outside world, and even of his own body. In the end the only thing he could not doubt was that he was doubting, that he was thinking. Hence his famous, or infamous, conclusion: *Cogito ergo sum*. But, in the process of discovering his certainty he had split the world into two: into the extended things of space and the non-extended world of thought, into a public and a private realm. Others who followed, notably John Locke,[7] then built upon

6   An excellent, accessible account of Descartes' philosophy is offered by
     Brian Magee (1987: 76–95).
7   Markham, 2004: 4.

this division as a means of resolving the problem of religious diversity (which incidentally had also been part of Descartes' initial motivation). Faith could be safely consigned to the private realm in order to maintain the peace of the public, now effectively secular, realm. Yet, if the values of faith and personal conviction are thus insulated from the public world, then the resulting external world seems to emerge as a domain with no inherent values and is thus open to human manipulation and exploitation.

It is vital to understand, however, that whatever was achieved by this private-public split, it was *not* the removal of ideology from the public realm. Rather, the emergence of secular space simply served to render problematic a faith-based critique of the ideologies that inevitably took hold. Most prevalent of such ideologies in the Western world today is neo-liberal capitalism.

The Ideology of Neo-Liberalism

Jeremy Carrette and Richard King (2005: 4–12) argue that a fundamental shift has taken place, initially in British and North American culture, but then more globally, as a result of the deregulation of the markets begun by Margaret Thatcher and Ronald Regan in the 1980s. The upshot, Noreena Hertz (2001: 201–202) concurs, is that huge corporations and unaccountable supranational structures (such as the International Monetary Fund, World Bank and World Trade Organisation) now hold enormous financial power.

Economics becomes the new politics as 'government aban-
dons the attempt to give shape to society' (Rowan Williams,
2002) and instead pursues the guiding policy that what is
good for business is good for us all. Indeed this notion, that
whatever is good for the economy serves the common good,
has become an all-embracing tacit assumption that receives
relatively little public criticism. The 'successful' government
is thus the one that enables its national economy to gain a
greater market share, and increases the customer choice and
purchasing power of its citizens. The 'nation-state' is
replaced by the 'market-state' (Philip Bobbitt, 2003), even as
governments work to retain essential public services.[8]

Where once the language of science usurped that of theology as the dominant mode of discourse in society, now the
language of economics seems to hold that position (Carrette
and King, 2005: 5). Any doubts concerning this assertion can
easily be dispelled by making a rough calculation of what
proportion of the news media is devoted to economic matters. The entirety of the world, it seems, can be described as
being either in or out of recession. In consequence, the
notions of consumer choice, the benefits of market competition and the ideal of business efficiency come to shape much
of the social world, including health, and more particularly
for our purposes, education. Before moving to education
specifically, by way of facilitating a process of consciousness-
raising, we shall briefly examine the more general consequences of such economic reductionism.

8   This transformation was already predicted by Jean-François Lyotard
     (1984: 5) and points to a telling alignment between the interests of
     capitalism and certain 'postmodern' views of truth and value.

Economic Reductionism

One of the most telling indicators of the consequences of economics as the dominant lens through which to view the world is the negative pressure it applies to conceptual-isations of the human person. As Rowan Williams has observed, the model of person as consumer sees, 'the ideal human agent as an isolated subject confronting a range of options, each of which they are equally free to adopt for their own self-defined purposes' (2009a).

Notice how close we are here to Descartes, and the 'fantasy' (Williams, 2009b) that somehow we can escape the material order altogether, as the human person is defined essentially as will, or more accurately, as craving. The notion of person as consumer thus fragments the self into a concern for the immediate satisfaction of desire, and this outside of any clear account of how the self relates to others and to the wider environment. While a consumer society holds out the tanta-lising prospect of being able to define one's own goals in life through one's own choices, what degree of freedom is actu-ally on offer in an environment where the manipulation of desire (not just through advertising but via its contribution to a seductive tale of 'life-style') is common-place and where the range of choices is already pre-defined? Such 'choice' may thus actually make it harder to provide some sense of over-arching purpose that gives (rational) shape to a life, some clear, purposeful connection between the present and what comes before and after (Williams, 2002).

When economics becomes the primary category of social interaction, then the well-known advice *caveat emptor* spills over into a general suspicion about the other. If all is competition, then one must be on guard against being cheated. This may go some way to explaining the ubiquity of audit processes. Unchecked we must assume that the other is lazy, unproductive and not to be trusted. This leads to another difficulty. If it is the (economically) productive who are of value, then what of children (except as a lucrative source of consumer desire), the unemployed, the sick and the dying?

Finally, the market alone is unlikely ever to deliver on the equality of persons since it responds, by its very nature, to those who have the ability to pay. Moreover, the notion of, and incentive created by, wage-differentials are built into the very structure of its functioning.

> A stable disparity between economic returns according of the major classes is generic to capitalism, according to Giddens. Taxation schemes aimed at the redistribution of wealth have effected only marginal changes in relative differentials. (Gorringe, 1994: 48).

The Current Governmental View of Higher Education

Given the role of government in a 'market-state', as described above, and the fact that HEIs are clear beneficiaries of the public purse, one might predict with some confidence that, in the prevailing view of government, Higher Education is primarily of utilitarian value; it serves the interests of the national economy. This assumption would appear to find corroboration in the very recent transmutation of the Department of Innovation, Universities and Skills into that for Business, Innovation and Skills. 'Universities' have apparently lost their explicit place, subsumed by' Business'. Intriguingly, and promisingly, this predicted colonisation of universities by economic interests is very nearly the case, but not quite.

At the time of writing the promised Higher Education Framework, due in the autumn of 2009, is still awaited. In its absence, however, orientation may be found from two sources. First, the speech, *Higher Education and Modern Life*, given by Peter Mandelson, the Secretary of State for Business, Innovation and Skills;[9] and second the findings of the corresponding Parliamentary Select Committee (that had not yet been reconfigured in accordance with the change of departmental structure recorded above) which reported on Higher Education in August 2009.

Mandelson begins by effectively affirming the trajectory of development set out over twenty years before by the Conservative White Paper *Meeting the Challenge* (1987). This had sought to reform universities to better serve the needs of the economy. In answering the question, 'For what end?' of Higher Education, he speaks first of the economic role of a university:

9   Given at Birkbeck University on 27 July 2009.

I want the universities to focus more on commercial-
ising the fruits of their endeavour.

Yet, before this is expanded in fairly predictable ways, there
is a highly significant caveat:

> ... I do not believe that the function of a university is
> limited to – or even primarily about – economic out-
> comes. They are not factories for producing workers
> ... The case for a higher education system that invests
> in everything from classics[10] to quantum physics is a
> compelling one.

Mandleson offers four good reasons why Higher Education
may not be collapsed completely into economic interest. The
utility of knowledge is hard to predict in advance, knowledge is a legitimate end in itself, historical awareness and
critical thinking are essential skills for a 'rounded human
being', and the development of personal character and the
enhancement of economic competitiveness are hard to disen-
tangle in practice. He also later speaks of Higher Education's
broader role in serving the purpose of increasing social
mobility.

The summary provided of the Select Committee's findings
also includes, albeit in a rather less robust manner, a warning
against the final triumph of market forces. Ironically, however, its approach (which in fairness yields some legitimate
questions) falls all too easily into the genre of a consumer
report. Centring, as it did, on student experience, concerned

---

10   This cries out to be read against the now notorious comments of Charles
     Clark in 2003 which suggested that the study of medieval texts might be
     a luxury that could no longer be afforded.

for 'value for money' and appealing for a greater degree of standardisation (of both information to guide choice and in the measure of degree outcomes) it fits neatly into the mindset of a customer in search of a consumable product. Yet, and here is the moment of critique, the Committee found the suggestion, deriving from the 'culture at the top of Higher Education', that 'it was possible to justify academic standards with a market structure' wholly inadequate. It was not prepared to see the continued success of British universities at attracting international students as evidence that standards had been maintained. Instead it sought reassurance concerning an absolute measure of degree standard.

In the argument that follows we will wish to take seriously these chinks of light shining through the armour of economic ascendancy. Church HEIs have good reason, as we shall explore, for wanting to take Mandleson at his word.[11]

What has happened to Higher Education?

The transformation of British Higher Education from an elite pursuit to one of mass participation, accomplished over the last twenty years or so, has not been without effect. Perhaps not enough will be said in what follows about the positive consequences of this change, particularly in enabling a wider

11 2010 will, of course, see a change of Government be that Labour, Conservative or Liberal Democrat. Searching for the same invitation to challenge the economic reduction of education will continue to be vital if the argument of this chapter is accepted.

section of the population to participate in its transformative opportunities. As one who has worked in university chaplaincy and academic life for the past fifteen years, I have witnessed firsthand, many times over, what this means for individual lives. Yet there has been the general pretence that what has been achieved is the offering of the *same* experience to a *greater* number of people. This is manifestly not the case. The inevitable consequences of a shrinking unit of resource as the sector expanded, combined with the ever encroaching ideology of neo-liberalism, have taken their toll on the nature of what is available. Loughlin (2004: 120) puts the matter starkly:

> Toward the latter part of the twentieth century, British university education ceased to be about the formation of informed and critical sensibilities, and became a means for maximising earning potential.

To put the matter thus, however, is unhelpfully to polarise the situation into an 'old' and 'new' which simply stand in static opposition It is better, I wish to argue, to see that matter in terms of a form of 'climate change'.

In response to the incipient effects of 'global warming', and its re-patterning of climactic zones around the globe, species can already be observed to be shifting their customary sites of occupation (and, at the extreme end of the phenomenon, finding a loss of suitable ecological niche, facing extinction). Where I reside in Kent, the local wine-makers have been conspicuous beneficiaries. The disappearance of vast flocks of starlings an unwelcome loss. A parallel phenomenon has been occurring in Higher Education. As the environment created by successive waves of Government legislation has had its effect, some elements of the 'old' model have become rarely observed or have even disappeared. New modes of practice and understanding have taken their place, and the balance of the remainder has changed. Thus it is not that a crudely instrumentalist model of Higher Education has simply ousted one where 'the formation of informed and critical sensibilities' took centre stage, it is rather that the environment has become more hostile to the survival of the latter; it still persists if one is prepared to look. What follows then can be understood as a brief overview of the consequences of this changing climate, more particularly a concise natural history of new 'species' of outlook and practice appearing in our HEIs.

One possible place to observe the crystallization of these alterations is to consider what it means to have introduced a 'National Student (satisfaction) Survey', the results of which are published in the form of a league table. Let us be clear; this is not to suggest that there is no place for a legitimate feedback mechanism which has always been part of good education, let alone to suggest that this Survey by itself has caused the changes observed. Rather, as symptomatic of such changes, this Survey may be used as a heuristic tool.

Students, who might have formerly understood themselves as primarily *members* of an academic community are now encouraged to view themselves as *customers*[12] of a

---

12   It could be argued, of course, that the most decisive factor in this change of perspective is caused by the increased fees required of students. While this is certainly an unarguable factor, it need not, in an appropriate environment, detrimentally change the relationship

'higher education outlet'.[13] Students thus come to be seen as purchasers of degrees, primarily viewed as the route to higher income potential, thus making financial sense of the 'investment' required. Worse, they become the passive consumers of a 'student experience' that is expected to be provided without any direct contribution from the students themselves.

The relationship between HEIs becomes principally that of competitors. In this new context the need arises for universities to become organisations that are 'completely market orientated' deriving 'from an acknowledgement of university provision as a consumer-focussed service, the rise of the competitive market place and the subsequent struggle to achieve marketing advantage through the building of brand personality' (Stamp, 2001: 158). Accordingly, pedagogy becomes constrained to the popular, to the marketable. Academic disciplines, formed by long tradition, are raided to procure attractive morsels served as easily-digestible modules. The immediate satisfaction of desire, the hallmark of a consumer mindset, thus risks breaking the integrity of an arduous journey that seeks to build skill upon skill in an ascending ladder of competence. The discipline required to be formed into an intellectual tradition is abandoned as the 'now' of present contentment comes to usurp the place of a cumulative journey towards a hard won future of intellectual formation. The result, if one is not very careful, is the reduction of education to entertainment. That this is occurring can

between students and the university community of which they are a part.

13   Roberts (2002: 88).

may be invoked from the form taken by some student assessment of their courses. Naomi Klein (2001: 98) offers a complementary perspective from the North American context which seems increasingly to ring true on this side of the Atlantic:

> Many professors speak of the slow encroachment of the mall mentality ... They tell of students filling out their course-evaluation forms with all the smug self-righteousness of a tourist responding to a customer-satisfaction form at a large hotel chain.

In a context where what appears to matter most is the subsequent earning potential of graduates, and the contribution they can make to the success of the economy, the method and content of study becomes less important than the input it can make to their 'employability'. Carrette and King (2005: 165-6) are not so far from the mark when they write:

> In the UK context of higher education...it hardly matters now *what* you teach or even *how* you teach it, as long as you can provide the appropriate documentation to demonstrate that your courses can be mapped in terms of supposedly generic and transferable skills, deemed necessary for a flexible workforce.[14] The subject being studied becomes reduced to its utilitarian basics, and degrees become little more than training courses for 'tooling up' the workforce to meet the competitive demands of global capitalism.

---

14 Cf. Roberts (2002: 97–98) and his notion that modules now function in an enclosed economy of meaning without effective reference to a reality (which might reasonably be the prime object of study) beyond.

As Augustine of Hippo observed long ago, in relation to the pagan universities of his day, they exist to serve the purposes of vanity: to gain better employment and obtain self-promotion.[15] Likewise the Church of England report *Aiming Higher* (2005: 3.2) endorsed the view that there had been a worrying shift in potential motivation for entering Higher Education from an 'ideal of self-sacrifice in the common interest' towards that of 'self-interest'.

What then of the institutions themselves? How has the serving of student need in a competitive market affected them? Roberts (2002) offers a far-reaching and brutally honest account of his own experience as an academic wishing to subscribe to the ideal of the 'natural rights of the life of the mind' (Bonhoeffer) in a context of profound and enforced change. In particular, he is highly critical of the increasingly common line-management model of organisation within universities which risks reducing the notion of 'academic freedom' to a sham.

> [U]nless the definition of academic freedom includes certain rights to organise the production and distribution of knowledge in the setting of 'natural rights of the life of the mind', then that freedom is nominal and vacuous. (2002: 92–93)

What lies behind this strident assertion? In a context of competitive financial struggle for survival, HEIs have raced to adapt to the imposed requirements of government at a pace that has had to bypass much of the previous internal democratic process. Managerialist fiat has thus closed down upon

---

15   The observation of D'Costa (2005: 2).

the very activity of critical questioning and independence of thought that has traditionally been understood as the essence of a university's nature. In consequence, academics can feel as though they no longer 'own the means of production' of their own goods — teaching and research. Forced to comply with general programme specifications, required to seek permission to effect even minor changes to validated modules, a degree of alienation from their vocation to be courageous seekers after truth in critical relation to the accepted understandings of reality is the inevitable consequence. The university is thus changed from within, transferring its gaze from a concern that ultimately transcends the immediate world of (currently assumed) utilitarian objectives, to that very world itself. What is lost is 'a commitment to the integrity of the university as the realm of the critical mind' (Roberts, 2002: 89).

For the sake of clarity in establishing what is at stake, perhaps the reader will indulge an extreme analogy. Disneyland Paris boasts an exact replica of nineteenth century gold mine buildings originating from the 'old West'. Its purpose is to act as the entry point to a pretended runaway train ride: 'Big Thunder Mountain'. The gold mine, for all its meticulous reconstruction, is not real except in this sense; it is there to add verisimilitude to the pretence and so enhance the joy of the ride.

Using this as an example of the nature of theme park simulacrums, we might advance the following definition concerning them: they are something with a reality that only exists for the sake of, and in the presence of, their customers.

Turning now from Disneyland to the matter at hand, if the 'reality' of a university only exists for the sake of its students and its research 'customers',[16] if it has no inherent identity and purpose into which others are invited to participate, no sense of an overarching intrinsic vocation, then it comes close to being but the theme park simulacrum of a university. It becomes an institution which appears to have all the accoutrements of a university yet lacks its defining operation. At the far end of the 'climate change' process, as the Armageddon from which we can yet turn back, lies this ugly prospect: academics who can no longer teach critical thinking because the institution of which they are a part has become fully colonized by the immediate demands of a society over against which it no longer possesses any critical distance.

Economics Reconsidered

The current economic purview has its limit. For all the pervasiveness of the neo-liberal perspective, of a 'free market', the ideal of perpetual economic growth, competitiveness as a route to efficiency and the attendant paradigm of consumerism, there is a horizon within which this ideology is already being called into serious public question. That horizon is the 'ecological crisis'. Global warming and attendant climate

---

16   Monbiot (2001: 281–301) offers an account of the increasing link between university research and corporate interest. He concludes: 'Business now stands as a guard dog at the gates of perception. Only the enquiries which suit its needs are allowed to pass.' (301).

change, the pollution of land, ocean and atmosphere, water shortages and an unprecedented extinction rate are its hallmarks. Yet while this crisis ostensibly manifests itself in the physical realm, it is fundamentally a crisis of human values. More, as Jürgen Moltmann recognises, it is a 'religious' crisis in the sense that it concerns that in which, particularly in the Western world, men and women place their trust.

> The crisis we are experiencing is therefore not just an 'ecological crisis', nor can it be solved by purely technical means. A change in convictions and basic values is as necessary as a change in attitudes in life and life-style (Moltmann, 1989: 53).

Set against the consequences for the earth, our economic ambitions are revealed for what they are. The unfettered demand for 'progress' and 'growth', the desire for an ever-increasing standard of life (judged by the range of goods and services one can command) is revealed as nothing less than a concealed death-drive (Moltmann, 1992: 97).

The kinds of attitudes and behaviours that are going to be required to return us to a path towards life run profoundly contrary to the consumerist model of economic and politics. A fundamental recognition of our radical dependence upon the ecosystem of the earth combines with the need for international cooperation at an unprecedented level to demonstrate the hopeless fantasy of the autonomous agent of desire that is the anthropological model at the heart of neo-liberalism. Only by the restriction of certain sorts of consumption (Williams, 2002) can the crisis be averted, as the indisputable finitude of the earth sets limits on our ambitions. Already the Western standard of living cannot be universalised (Moltmann, 1999: 93). The only alternative will be a radically different understanding of 'quality of life'.

Awareness of the 'ecological crisis' helps put economics in its place. It reveals that economics — which we might define as a 'system of exchange' of goods and services often involving money — is itself set in a much more fundamental 'system of exchange' that it cannot ignore: that of life itself. The utilisation of food and (for us) oxygen, the removal of waste and reproduction are part of a life-process that spreads out laterally beyond the individual to the ecosystem inhabited, and temporally through the four billion year history of evolution. If the market economy is but a sub-set of life, it cannot, therefore, become the meaning or exhaustive measure of life.

Grand as this vision of the all-embracing system of life may seem, within a theological perspective it is still too parochial. One could argue that a 'system of exchange' is not just to be found within the realm of creation, but also characterises the highest reality, that of God. For according to Christian insight, God exists as Trinity, as an exchange of love between Persons grounded in indestructible life. The Father's eternal generation of the Son and the Spirit, this movement of generative love, is reciprocated by the Son's loving response to the Father mediated through the Spirit, and revealed supremely in the cross. God does not exist apart from this eternal circling movement of love given and love received. It is as the (freely willed) outworking of this love that creation comes to be: its existence grounded in God's generative love, its redemption in God's responding love. Stepping back a little, we can thus say that loving exchange characterises the being of God, enables the existence of the created realm, and so finds its own analogy in the intricate ecological web of life of which we are a part. For God and for the world the Spirit must therefore be understood as the 'Spirit of exchange', which is only another of saying what the Christian tradition has long said: the Spirit is the 'Giver of life'.[17]

Once 'economics' is understood first and foremost in this way, certain forms of exchange begin to look aberrant. Forms of exchange which move away from being mutually supportive and enriching, which reduce the other to merely instrumental value, and which work against the sustaining of life rather than for it, must be judged as seriously deficient. More particularly, a neo-liberal economic system which is leading towards the 'ecological crisis', and thus is in danger of permanently harming the basis of life, is exposed as flawed. If a system of economics does not serve life, it does not deserve support.

Distinctiveness as a Form of Exchange

We return now to the question with which we began, that of the distinctiveness of a Church HEI. There have been many attempts, perhaps most recently with *A Guide to Governance* (2007, C.1.3), to enumerate a list of 'distinctives'. I wish to argue that while this instinct is not wrong, it is of itself insufficient. Christian distinctiveness does not *sufficiently* lie in

---

17   The Niceno-Constantinopolitan Creed of 381CE.

one, or a combination, of the following: the presence of posts covered by a Genuine Occupational Requirement (GOR); the particular constitution of the Governing Body; the presence of a chaplaincy team, chapel and regular Christian worship; the presence of conspicuous Christian signs and symbols; the name of an institution; a subject mix biased towards the public services; the presence of a department of (Christian) theology. The reason for this assertion is not just that these features could be accidentally replicated in any HEI. Nor may we escape the problem concerning such a list by turning distinctiveness into the form of a 'we must, they may'. Rather, the *sine qua non* of distinctiveness, I wish to argue, lies not in attributes but in process.

An analogy may be helpful. Assuming nothing untoward has happened, the engine of the car you parked last time it was used contains all the required components to function: pistons; combustion chambers; ignition system; fuel delivery system; crankshaft and the rest. But their presence alone is insufficient to constitute a useful engine. What is required is that these components come to serve the enabling of a living *process*: the controlled combustion of fuel and air. In the absence of this process, all one has is a hefty lump of metal and plastics, or, put rather less pejoratively, a favourable site where the process of combustion *might* take place.

In a Church HEI, there is a parallel situation. The list of 'distinctives' serves to delineate, at most, a site favourable for the occurrence of a process which holds the key to meaningful distinctiveness. That process is the creative interaction (form of exchange) between the meta-narrative of the Gospel of Jesus Christ and the ideologies of the day, such that the

Gospel can contribute towards the decision-making and shaping of the institution. In the absence of this process of exchange, the presence of any number of static 'distinctives' will not guarantee a distinctive institution. To put it plainly, they will be as helpful as an engine that will not fire.

Another way of expressing this proposal is to say that a Church HEI is one in which there is a *public theology* concerning its purpose and operation. The word 'public' is vital. Earlier we examined the legacy of Descartes and Locke in which faith, and the perspective it offers, became a matter for the private realm alone. In addition to this first privatisation of religion, Carrette and King (2005: 15-17) have identified a second phase that builds upon the first.

> In the late twentieth century, however, there has been a second form of privatisation that has taken place ... It can be characterised as the wholesale *commodification* of religion, that is the selling-off of religious buildings, ideas and claims to authenticity in service to the industrial/corporate profit and the provision of a particular worldview and mode of life, namely corporate capitalism ... Religion is rebranded as 'spirituality' in order to support the ideology of capitalism.

Spirituality is a notoriously difficult term to define. Carrette and King thus provide a short history of the ideation (2005: 30–53) along with a precise anatomy of the kind of corporate spirituality they have in their sights (2005: 21–22). We do not need to follow the complexity of their analysis here provided we are alert to the danger of attempting to substitute the task of public theology for a commitment to a general encouragement of the spirituality of staff and students. Such an individualised, and essentially private spirituality, will have little, if anything, to say to the defining structure of a Church HEI, and worse, in the context of the overall argument of this chapter, may actually serve the interest of, rather than challenge, the commodification of education. It is thus vital that chaplains are not reduced to sources of individual pastoral counselling and to managers of religious resource (for individuals). To do so would be to quarantine the tradition they represent away from the public functioning of the institution.

What then would foster the kind of public theology envisaged? First, the institution needs to be home to a living Christian community where the meta-narrative of the Gospel is honoured and practiced, where it is authenticated and lived.

Secondly, the institution will require a department of theology whose teaching, research and general presence provides the academic legitimacy for a public theological discourse that serves the Kingdom of God (not merely the historical and comparative analysis of texts with a religious content).

Thirdly, there is a need to ensure that those who would not hold the positions they do in the absence of a particular faith commitment (for example, Head of Institution, chaplain(s), members of the Governing Body) can readily converse such that their deliberations might contribute to the shaping of the institution. It must be said in passing that this will prove much harder to achieve if the chaplaincy team are located in Student Services (as is beginning to happen) rather than reporting directly to the Principal or Vice Chancellor. The ensuing conversations would, in effect, form the explicit nucleus of what might be termed a 'Foundation Community' around which a broader, more implicit, community could form. This 'Foundation Community' would seek to mobilise successfully those within the institution for whom the Christian Gospel constitutes a meaningful point of orientation (which is not quite the same as those who necessarily subscribe to and practice the Christian Faith).

Fourthly, the presence of a clear public theology would provide the required context in which the Christian signs and symbols of the institution, together with its symbolic geography (such as the size and location of the chapel) could speak an authentic counter-cultural word. That is, for example, such public theology would provide a context in which the viewing of a cross would become more than the seeing of a Christian 'logo'; it might become, rather, an invitation to consider what self-sacrifice in the common good means in a time of consumer virtue.

Fifthly, a public theology needs to be sustained by a continuing relationship with the broader community of the church of which the institution is a part. Without this nurturing interest by the wider ecclesiastical body, a body of public standing, there is the danger that the theological voice within the Church HEI will collapse back into an expression of private preference without wider claim to attention.

Finally, this public theology must take its place in policy documents, it must be voiced at committee meetings, it must be the subject of occasional open discussions, and it must reach to the Council of Church Universities and Colleges and the Joint Advisory Committee for the Church Universities and Colleges sponsored by the Higher Education Funding

Council for England (HEFCE). In short, it must become part of the common 'currency' of the exchange of ideas.

It must be underlined that what is envisaged here does not seek to close down debate nor exclude the views of those within the institution (and beyond) who may not be able to subscribe to this public theology in its entirety. Rather, quite the reverse: by defining the distinctive identity of a Church HEI in terms of a process of exchange, an interchange of perspectives in which the Christian Gospel should have a guaranteed but not exclusive place, what should ensue is a greater degree of conversation between voices from different viewpoints. In other words, it is envisaged as a way of securing and enhancing the democratic functioning of the institution.[18] Moreover, it would legitimate such discussion taking place on the basis of values rather than pragmatic expediency. It is hoped, therefore, that these proposals will meet the test of the 'reality check' performed above.

Serving the Economy of Life

So much, then, for the existence of a public theology, and the structural process that sustains it; what may be said about its content? At one level, of course, this must be a matter for each institution given the immediate concerns of its time and place. But there is also the need for a collective vocation,

18 Here I concur with both Markham (2004: 11) and Higton (2006: 21–22) who both see conversation as one of the essential marks of a university informed by Christian insights.

especially as regards the recent transformation of Higher Education. The Church HEIs, as was said at the outset, have the opportunity to speak a word that not only actualises their distinctiveness, but also holds a public relevance for the whole Higher Education sector.

Education, it might be said, is about enabling one to take one's place in the world. But here everything depends upon which world is in mind. Is this the world of financial transaction, or that of ecological vulnerability, or even one open to the 'sacred canopy' of the Trinitarian God? From the theological standpoint, anything less than a willingness to set one's view of the world within the perspective of God is but an abstraction from the whole. It is to foreclose on the possibility of relating to the fullness of reality. Moreover, for the purposes of our considerations here, it would be to foreclose on a perspective that can help prevent education from collapsing into a utilitarian means to an end which is not in the interests of even the most avowedly secular university. Education then, in its broadest sense, can be understood as learning how to live in relation to all that is.

> We could say ... that the proper job of a university is to grow our nervous system; to allow us to put out new nerves so as to be sensitive in new ways to the world around us ... to be more responsive. (Higton, 2006: 11)

Education is about coming to understand one's existence within a total ecology. It is, as Rowan Williams (2009b) has stated, fundamentally about relationship: relationship with others, with the whole environment and with God.

This ambition at relationship takes us back to an earlier understanding of reason. It takes us back behind modernity to a 'concept of reason as the organ of perception and participation (methexis)' (Moltmann, 1985: 2). Here one knows not in order to dominate or control, to manipulate and turn to a profit (the more modern sense), but rather to participate in the reality in which one finds oneself, to participate in the world and to understand oneself in relation to God. In short, the educated use of reason becomes learning how to take one's place in life. Against this measure, and particularly in relation to the 'ecological crisis':

> We need to question a very great deal of what has passed as rationality in our habits of production and consumption for the last century. (Williams, 2009b)

And this means in turn, questioning the ideology of neo-liberalism that seems to be increasingly shaping Higher Education in Britain.

In one sense there is nothing wrong in preparing students to take their place in the economy. But we must ask: Which economy and for what ends? An unreflective emphasis on the 'employability' of our graduates might mean preparing them to contribute to an existing economy that is working against the long-term interests of life. Do we not rather wish them to have the critical ability to call the present in question, the courage and vision to strive for an alternative future even as they have to cooperate, to some degree, with the *status quo*. Our students need to be able to inhabit 'both this world and the next' — the present world of work and the new world of work which, we can at least hope, will be better in its relation to the ecology of life and social justice. In other words, such critical preparation provides a set of 'transferable skills' that are likely to have a longer period of relevance than those tightly constrained to the alleged needs of the present moment.

If we wish our students to escape the consumerist paradigm, then their experience of Higher Education must be in contradistinction to it. Without losing the new consideration of the variety of ways in which people learn, without losing an appropriate accommodation to student needs, we urgently need to turn them from (passive) consumers of education back into (active) members of an academic community - into those who take responsibility for the shape of their own 'student experience'. Overly prescriptive 'learning outcomes' that shape 'pre-packaged' modules of learning need to allow room for the reciprocal and irreducibly unpredictable business of exploration of the new. Education understood in this way can never be comprehended within the category of a product to be bought and sold because it spills over the package that seeks to contain it. This inability to contain makes sense when education is seen for what it is; it is part of the essential matter of life.

The research life of the institution must also be such as to call the existing models of society into question, as part of its broader quest to discover what is the real 'real world' as opposed to the various ideological constructions of it which work in the favour of the few and the (already) powerful. 'The truth shall make you free' (John 8: 32) lies at the heart of what it means to be a university and demonstrates why research-led teaching is so valuable. As the site of such activity an HEI can genuinely serve the *common* good as well as working to secure the democratic freedom of thought that underpins a consensual society.

Trying to turn around the recent trends in the nature of Higher Education will not be easy. It will be like trying to overcome the vast inertia of an oil tanker at sea that has already settled into a straight line course. But there lies at the heart of each Church HEI a resource which, if connected to the institution by the kind of public theology described above, can challenge the ruling influences over Higher Education in the interests of life: the chapel.

The Trinitarian pattern of exchange, between Father, Son and Holy Spirit, is rooted in love and thus in gift. And the notion of gift has the ability to radically undercut that of meritocracy which, while an appropriate element of a Church HEI (in the marking of student work and as the criterion of staff promotion) cannot be allowed to have last word. This is because there will be an important and non-negotiable sense in which the intrinsic value of each person cannot rest on the quality of their performance, but follows directly and simply from God's prior relation with them. This idea, that it is not possible to draw a straight line from performance to value, is one key way in which the Kingdom of God challenges the workings of a market economy[19]

Economic value reduces time and space to the calculable, to the easily *accountable*. The celebration of Christian worship

19   Cf. '[T]he market tempts us to view the world in terms of values. It produces a 'critical frame of mind' that reduces everything which is good, true and beautiful to a formal value based on usefulness and substitutability, flattening all hierarchies to formal equivalences.' (Long, 2000:262).

calls this into question in the name of gift. In other words, the chapel can become the source of a liberating notion of space and time that speaks of an alternative order of things.

Economic time is essentially homogeneous 'clock time', indifferent to the qualities of events that unfold within it. Every hour is precisely the same as every other. If one is paid by the hour the assumption is that each hour is equally productive. But this is alienating from human experience. It ignores our different perceptions of the rate at which time passes. It takes no account of the time of inspiration and the time of the unproductive blank. It squeezes out the variations caused by the cyclical rhythms of body and nature, of sickness and health, of season and phase. The re-humanizing of time requires a kairological concept of the appropriate time,[20] the fitting time, the right time. The Christian festivals that punctuate the academic year, and still provide its shape, suggest that time is not so interchangeable. They thus suggest that life has a rhythm that cannot be constrained, nor fully comprehended, by the language of economic productivity. By allowing the celebration of Christian festivals to interrupt the rhythm of the life of the HEI — to be (potentially at least) community events, not hidden away as a purely private option — there is the opportunity to challenge the prevailing culture.[21]

20   Cf. Moltmann (1985: 118).
21   This raises, of course, the question how easy it is for members of the institution to attend such celebrations. Is there an all-embracing expectation that members should remain productive and so 'do not have the time'? Are members located at some distance from the Chapel, as may well be the case in a multi-campus institution? Finding ways to overcome these potential obstacles will be vital if

Productive space is essentially homogeneous 'geometric' space, indifferent to that which fills it. Each square metre is the same as every other. A lecture booked for one room can be changed to another of equivalent space (and facilities). But this too is alienating from human experience. It overlooks the effects of space and architecture on meaning and inspiration. It disregards the effect of context on mood and self-understanding. The re-humanizing of space requires an ecological concept of the appropriate space.[22] A chapel — as long as it is not used as merely another economic resource — provides justification for the notion that not all space is interchangeable. On any audit of space usage it should show up as anomalously underutilized (even when full!); that is its job.

This combination of understandings of space and time can lead to a particular sense of the priority of being in which the place of striving and performance are radically conditioned. Life is seen once more as gift, holi-day becomes the meaning of life, the anticipation of what will prove to be of eternal significance. The incessant demand for performance is liberatingly conditioned and it becomes possible to learn again how to live. This is education as contemplation which is markedly distinct from the utilitarian education for capability.

the everyday functioning of a Church HEI is not to unwittingly undermine the potential of its counter-cultural witness.
22   See Moltmann (1985: 142–5).

Conclusion

Emerging from relatively humble beginnings, the majority of surviving Church HEIs are now universities in their own right. They have emerged into this company at an opportune moment, for, contained within their founding tradition, are the seeds of renewal for a Higher Education sector that is in danger of becoming captive to the ideology of neo-liberalism. The Church HEIs, if they have the courage and the conviction, certainly possess a source from which to speak another, better word. How they choose to act will be nothing less than a test of Christian leadership. The Church HEIs are not required to hold all the answers as to precisely how Higher Education might be reformed to enable it to rediscover its calling to search for truth in the service of life, but surely the vantage point afforded them by their founding tradition demands the asking of a set of searching, critical questions. These are questions of relevance to the whole Higher Education sector which, if it is to be true to itself, must press beyond the immediate to the ultimate — an essentially theological vocation. For the Church HEIs then, finding distinctiveness can coincide with the discovery of relevance as they practise their distinctive vocation, that of recalling Higher Education to the service of the economy of life.[23]

23 I would like to acknowledge the encouragement offered by my colleague Dr Ralph Norman in the work of expanding my original presentation into this chapter. In particular he directed me to a range of

References

Bobbitt, Philip (2003), *The Shield of Achilles: War, Peace and the Course of History*, London: Penguin.

Brighton, Trevor (ed.). (1989), *150 Years: The Church Colleges in Higher Education*, Chichester: West Sussex Institute of Higher Education.

Carrette, Jeremy and King, Richard (2005), *$elling Spirituality: The Silent Takeover of Religion*, London: Routledge.

D'Costa, Gavin (2005), *Theology in the Public Square: Church, Academy and Nation*, Malden, MA: Blackwell Publishing.

Descartes, René (1999), *Discourse on Method and Related Writings*, Translated by Desmond Clarke, London: Penguin.

Francis, Leslie (2004), 'Expectations of the Christian Campus: Ordinary Theology, Empirical Theology and Student Voices'. In *The Idea of a Christian University*, ed. Jeff Astley, Leslie Francis, John Sullivan and Andrew Walker, Milton Keynes: Paternoster.

Gorringe, Timothy (1994), *Capital and the Kingdom: Theological Ethics and the Economic Order*, London: SPCK.

Hertz, Noreena (2001), *The Silent Takeover*, London: William Heinemann.

Higton, Mike (2006), *Vulnerable Learning: Thinking Theologically about Higher Education*, Cambridge: Grove (E 140).

Klein, Naomi (2001), *No Logo*, London: Flamingo.

most helpful sources. In addition, thanks are due to Dr Terrance Clifford-Amos for suggested stylistic improvements to this text. I also wish to place on record the support of Professor Michael Wright, not least for inviting me to contribute to the debate about 'Christian Distinctiveness' at Canterbury Christ Church University for which the original kernel of the ideas presented here was developed.

Long, Stephen (2000), *Divine Economy: Theology and the Market*, London: Routledge.

Loughlin, Gerrard (2004), 'The University Without Question: John Henry Newman and Jacques Derrida on Faith in the University'. In *The Idea of a Christian University*, edited by Jeff Astley, Leslie Francis, John Sullivan and Andrew Walker, Milton Keynes: Paternoster.

Lyotard, Jean-François (1984), *The Postmodern Condition: A Report on Knowledge*, Manchester: Manchester University Press.

Magee, Brian (1987), *The Great Philosophers*, London: BBC.

Mandelson, Peter (2009), 'Higher Education and Modern Life' (Lecture given at Birkbeck University). http://www.dius.gov.uk/news_and speeches/speeches/peter-mandelson/universities

Markham, Ian (2004), 'The Idea of a Christian University'. In *The Idea of a Christian University*, edited by Jeff Astley, Leslie Francis, John Sullivan and Andrew Walker, Milton Keynes: Paternoster.

Moltmann, Jürgen (1985), *God in Creation: An Ecological Doctrine of Creation*, London: SCM.

Moltmann, Jürgen (1989), *Creating a Just Future*, London: SCM.

Moltmann, Jürgen (1992), *The Spirit of Life: A Universal Affirmation*, London: SCM.

Moltmann, Jürgen (1999), *God for a Secular Society: The Public Relevance of Theology*, London: SCM.

Monbiot, George (2001), *Captive State: The Corporate Takeover of Britain*, London: Pan.

Roberts, Richard (2002), 'The End of the University and the Last Academic'. In *Religion, Theology and the Human Sciences*, Cambridge: CUP.

Stamp, Rosemary (2001), 'A View from the Market Place'. In *The State of UK Higher Education*, Buckingham: SRHE & Open University Press.

Temple, William (1935), *Nature, Man and God*, London: Macmillan.

Thatcher, Adrian (2004), 'The Curriculum of a Christian University'. In *The Idea of a Christian University*, edited by Jeff Astley, Leslie Francis, John Sullivan and Andrew Walker, Milton Keynes: Paternoster.

Williams, Rowan (2002), The Richard Dimbleby Lecture. http://www.archbishopofcanterbury.org/839

Williams, Rowan (2009a), 'Ethics, Economics and Global Justice' (Lecture given at Cardiff University). http://www.archbishopofcanterbury.org/1301

Williams, Rowan (2009b), 'The Mission of the Anglican University in our Present Age' (Lecture given at Rikkyo University, Japan). http://www.archbishopofcanterbury.org/1301

Reports

(1994), *An Excellent Enterprise: The Church of England and its Colleges of Higher Education* . Church of England Board of Education.

(2001), *The Way Ahead : Church of England Schools in the New Millennium*. Church House Publishing, GS1406.

(2005), *Aiming Higher: Higher Education and the Church's Mission*. Church of England Board of Education.

(2006), *Mutual Expectations: The Church of England and Church Colleges/ Universities*. Church of England Board of Education.

(2007), *A Guide to Governance in Church Higher Education Institutions*. Council of Church Colleges and Universities.

(2009), *Students and Universities*. Report by the Select Committee for Innovation, Universities, Science and Skills. http://www. parliament.the-stationery-office.co.uk/pa/cm200809/cmselect /cmdius/170/17003.htm

Afterword

One of the things that any reader of this distinguished collection of essays will have noticed is the clarity with which one basic assumption is stated again and again. A Christian institution of Higher Education is not simply an HE institution that happens to have a particular history or even one that has a fairly secure place for religious practice and research in religious studies or theology; it is one that offers a distinctive perspective on education itself, at every level. And, in consequence, it is an institution that requires in its leadership a robust commitment to this perspective, at least as much as a visible religious allegiance — or rather, it will not separate religious allegiance from the issues of educational vision that will shape the institution's character.

Likewise, there is no shrinking away from the recognition that this can put Church-related HE institutions in some ways at odds with the prevailing ethos in education — with what the recent Cambridge Primary Review has called, starkly but justifiably, the official 'state philosophy' of education. The essays assembled here make it clear that the pervasive rhetoric about HE as primarily a context in which the

nation's economy can be strengthened by producing competitive and productive or 'innovative' workers and entrepreneurs cannot be decisive for Church-related bodies. Stefan
Collini wrote a few years ago about the corrupting language
of 'HiEdBiz' that has spread across so many policy documents, in and out of universities, language that suggests a
high level of collective amnesia about the nature of education. He will find some powerful allies in the authors of this
book for his concluding insistence that 'there are some kinds
of intellectual enquiry that are goods in themselves' (338)
and for his stout resistance to the notion that the needs of the
economy are the first thing to think about in justifying expenditure on HE.

But what exactly is this distinctive perspective which
impels such a challenge to received orthodoxy? As more than
one of the authors implies, it is essentially an affirmation of
what used to be called 'Christian humanism' – referring back
to the days when it was happily not taken for granted that
Christian faith was anti-human or that humanism was
anti-Christian. Christian humanism is a commitment to the
enrichment of human minds and imaginations in all possible
fields, on the grounds that humanity, made in the image of
God and restored in Jesus Christ, deserves all the attention,
cultivation and enlargement that can be found, so that the
reflection of God's abundant life and generosity can be
shown in an endless diversity of human settings. It is not a
perspective that privileges arts over sciences or the 'academic' over the practical, but it does insist that there are
going to be different sorts of excellence in human culture and
that all need appropriate nurturing and valuing. Equally it is

not a glibly optimistic picture of limitless possibilities for emancipated humans; it is serious about human history and its tragedies, and about the place of human beings in a complex universe that they do not control.

And in educational terms, this needs educational communities that are diverse, patient and flexible and that are also sceptical about merely functional accounts of the educational process; communities that are capable of conversations across disciplines, so that different styles of learning and enquiry are mutually understood as part of a coherent enterprise of human growth. This is not just a matter of realising each student's potential, the baseline for every educator's mission statement these days, but of realising a potential for grasping a vision that is neither mine alone nor my neighbour's alone — grasping the sense of a 'human project' to be shared in the economy of exchange which Jeremy Law so vividly portrays. And while this may not, in these terms, be a goal exclusive to religiously-inspired institutions, the bare fact is that without some foundational vision and narrative of what humanity is about, without the tools for diagnosing human hubris and self-delusion as well as human depth and creativity, the idea of a coherent 'project' will not long survive. In the aftermath of a few decades that have savaged most available secular versions of a comprehensive human story, religious belief remains one of the few available frameworks for such a task. A Church-related HE institution does not claim that it has a monopoly of wisdom and it does not apply dogmatic tests for its members; but it does and it must claim that wisdom is worth talking about and seeking and that the institution needs a critical mass within it of people

who are committed to the particular kind of wisdom that
Christian doctrine offers.

'A critical mass'; it is impossible to generalise about what
this may mean from one institution to another, but it is
instinctively plausible and has been persuasively argued in
these essays that without clear expectations of senior leadership such a critical mass will not be stable. In the language
which James Arthur borrows from Robert Benne, the slip-
page from an 'intentionally pluralist' community to an 'accidentally pluralist' one is not going to be arrested without a
leadership that is committed to maintaining living and
diverse connections with the parent tradition, and creating
opportunities for the institution to be of active service to that
tradition. What that can look like in practice, as well as in
theory, is admirably outlined here in the pieces from Joel
Cunningham (speaking from a rather more diverse and
sometimes more adventurous educational landscape than
that of the UK) and Gerald Pillay. This in turn means that the
Church can quite reasonably spell out its expectations, and
indeed must do so with clarity — just as the HE institution can
and should spell out its expectations of the Church in terms
of intelligent support (including support in defending its
educational vision and priorities). Several essays note how,
in the last few decades, unclarity about expectations from
both sides — and, it has to be admitted, a degree of indifference on both sides — has weakened the bonds between the
Church and the HE communities for which it has historically
been responsible. As with Church schools, there has now
been a notable revival of enthusiasm to make the relation

work; and, as with Church schools, this requires the Church
to invest in the support and training of good leadership.

Perhaps in the wake of the Dearing Report this is the single
most pressing challenge that the churches still have to follow
through. A great deal has been achieved in terms of institutional expansion and the renewal of Christian confidence;
what remains to be done is largely to do with spotting and
managing talent, training in appropriate ways and creating
structures that will help support individuals exercising
Christian leadership in educational institutions (importantly
but *not* exclusively Church-related ones, though that leads
into a much wider discussion about supporting the Christian
vocations of those who work outside the Church's own
schools, colleges and universities). Several institutions are
showing interest in developing further their work in equipping people to take leadership roles, and I should expect to
see a good deal of expansion in this area, and also, I hope, in
the wider Church's engagement with this. There are a number of crucial questions to be looked at in what should and
could be shared in the context of ministerial training, for
instance; there is wisdom to be shared in both directions
when these two worlds engage — not least given the nuanced
discussion of leadership, its possibilities and seductions, that
have been going on within ministerial training lately.

The human project is never an exclusively local or national
business. Part of what is opened up on this front for senior
leadership in a Church-related institution is something well
described by Janet Trotter, which has been developed also in
Christ Church, Canterbury, under Michael Wright's direction, and in other places; and that is a very distinctive inter-

national network, allowing students to be part of a larger global family, not exclusively academic. It is one of the aspects of HE in this context that most lends itself to discussion in terms of *transformative* educational practice — preparing students to live in a world whose horizons are not limited to their familiar cultural surroundings, let alone simply to earning a comfortable living within those surroundings. But this also means that a senior leader in such a community needs herself or himself to be aware of the world Church and its possibilities; and once again, there is a challenge to the Church to help keep these global relationships alive and well and to inform people about them. Good HE practice in this area is bound up with the health of the Church across the globe: it is one of many areas where the current problems of the Anglican Communion need to be seen within the broadest possible picture of the mission and responsibilities of Christ's people.

So these essays leave us with both encouragement and questioning. It is possible to imagine a fully professional, diverse, creative institution of Higher Education thoroughly grounded in the Christian faith, fully attentive to its doctrines and practices but completely credible in the world of non-believers and half-believers because of its depth of humane vision; an institution capable of offering reasoned challenge to the sometimes misdirected expectations which HE in Britain seems to be suffering from, and backing that challenge with manifestly good practice. The institutions mentioned in this book and the leadership that has already been shown by its authors represent a remarkable story of how Church-related HE recovered its nerve and its distinctive cutting edge. There is an enormous amount to build on. At the same time, we are left under no illusions about the difficulties. The cultural climate is not friendly, and the levels of indifference or suspicion about religion in society in general and sadly in some parts of the educational establishment in particular are worrying. The pool of religiously committed talent to develop for leadership is not that large. Yet no one can doubt that we now have a powerful vision coming together in this field and that the intellectual and organisational energy shown in Church HE institutions in recent years has been outstanding. The hope must be that the Church itself will continue to broaden and deepen its support for these communities where its own service to society is so ably taken forward, confident — as all these essays suggest — that a vigorous and potentially radical partnership will unfold for the health of the educational establishment as well as the good of the Church itself.

+ Rowan Cantuar:

Lambeth Palace, Advent 2009